Extraordinary Living

...above the
Ordinary

by

Pamala Chestnut

Extraordinary Living...above the Ordinary
by Pamala Chestnut

Cover Design by Margo Bush

Published by Bush Publishing P.O. Box 692082
Tulsa, Oklahoma 74169-2082
www.BushPublishing.com

Printed in the USA

To Troy

For loving all of us
as if we were yours from the beginning;
Apryl, Aaron, Amy & Neil, Chelsea, Jewel,
Brandon, Brad, Emma and Micah,
and your wife, Pamala

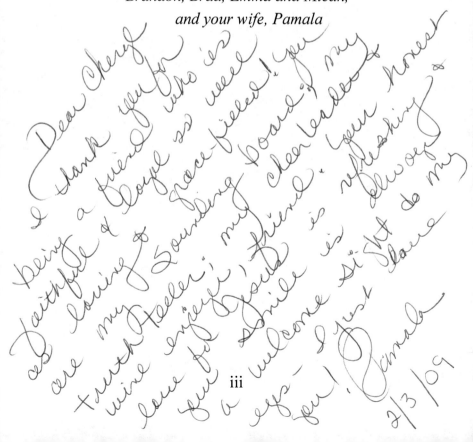

Foward

"Pamala Chestnut is herself an extraordinary human being, bringing together a life history of overcoming in almost every arena of life. She is not only an extraordinary speaker, writer, and coach to hundreds whom she has inspired, she has been, by turns, a pastor's daughter, a pastor's wife, a reigning beauty queen, a sought after worship contributor and ministry innovator, and a celebrity on talk shows, radio and television. She has gained her status not because of the positions she has held or the awards she has won, but because of the scars she has overcome-- physically, mentally, and emotionally--in her journey to becoming one of America's most beloved Christian women. Let Pamala inspire you to the next level of the life you have always wanted...You will not be disappointed."

Lance Lee, PhD
Executive Coach and Consultant
Director, Center for Relationship,
Silicon Valley, California

Extraordinary

In the pages that follow I hope to instill in you the determination to seize an extraordinary life. What is extraordinary? It is determining to do whatever it takes to move past ordinary. Anyone can coast through life being...ordinary. I ask you to dare to dream bigger, larger than ordinary, choose to be different. Take life to the next level; work toward excellence every chance you get. When taking on a new task, master it before moving on to the next. It is better to do a few things extraordinary than many things just so, so. When it comes to taking care of your body, do more than just get by. Be disciplined, eat right and exercise, manage stress in your life and take time to relax and rest. Let your love be unmatched! Forgive graciously. Give generously. Be the friend to others that you have always wanted to have. Push yourself when you feel uncomfortable with a new project or idea until it becomes easy. Never let go of your dreams, and always dream big.

It will take courage to move from ordinary to extraordinary, but you will not regret it. Others long to see something to emulate, a hero to look up to, a mentor to follow. Be that to someone. Our world needs strong leaders leading the right way. Decide to take your place and fulfill the destiny meant for you and you alone. God has always had great plans for your life. I challenge you to move from ordinary living to extraordinary living, in every arena of life. Through hard circumstances, through tough personal assessment, through accepting others, as well as yourself, through personal growth in work and marriage, through an intimate daily encounter with God. Be extraordinary!

Blessings on your adventure,

Pamala

Table of Contents

Chapter 1

Extraordinary Cannot be Faked

Painful experiences in my life have forced a change in me forever. I have now gained true strength of heart, soul and body, whereas before I tried to appear to be a superhero, complete with a big red "S" on my chest. No one knew that under my superhero suit resided a scared wimp. In true hero form I pressed ahead regardless of the crisis, never revealing my true identity. I was compelled to be superhuman - it was my trademark. I was, after all, the daughter of a minister; a 4.0 student; wife and a mother; the friend who would never let you down; the volunteer who would say yes without much thought of the cost; and many other sacrificial accomplishments validating the super S on my chest even more. I was determined to exude absolute perfection, meeting everyone's expectations with my superhuman powers, which by the way, I really never had.

I almost pulled it off

Surprisingly I got through many incredible challenges. It looked as if I was pulling it off, but in reality I was weakening with each new crisis. Still I refused to remove the big red "S" from my chest. I felt if I appeared weak it would be a bad reflection on my faith and on God's strength. I had a lot to learn about appearances, and how inadequate they are when it comes to endurance. Endurance is what it takes to get through a long haul. It will take endurance if you want to live a life above the ordinary. To endure means "to suffer patiently without yielding; to last; to continue in existence." Endurance is not developed quickly or effortlessly. Any façade of super humanness has to go. You cannot fake endurance. If you try faking it you just won't last. Endurance is an inside job and that was the problem; inside was hard for me to find. I had spent my time perfecting the big red "S" on the outside for all to see. No one, including me, was looking inside. However I finally was faced with a crisis that hurt so much, was so deep and frightening, so hopeless that I was forced to rip the big red "S" from my chest. This left a hole in my humanity, creating an entrance to the inner most part of me. It was a painful process, but in time, I discovered the inside - my soul.

Finding the inside of me is what saved all of me. I didn't realize that the big red "S" was really a prison from which I needed to be set free. Although I would never have chosen suffering to gain my freedom, the truth is, I now am free. It did not happen overnight and there were days I wanted to wimp out. I even wished for my fairy godmother to come with her magic wand and change me instantly, but no wand appeared. Instead I rested and sought God for new courage. I found I was going to have to work at this soul-finding thing. God, not a fairy godmother, would be there to strengthen my steps, *but it was my job to take the steps.* I have listed some of these and trust they can help you as you develop the endurance you will need for your long haul.

1. Seek solitude. As long as there is distraction you will not have the discipline it takes to look deep within. I went away for a week by myself. I rented a cabin in the Santa Cruz Mountains. I took food, my Bible and a journal. No phone, no television, no computer, no work, and the most difficult for me...no people. I am a people addict. Yes, there is such a thing. I despise being alone. But I needed to be alone so I would be forced to talk to myself.

2. Talk to yourself. Ask questions you would ask someone you want to know intimately.

- How would you describe yourself?

- What is the best thing about you?

- What is your greatest failure?

- What do you want said about you when you are gone? Will it be said?

- Who do you trust? Why?

- Who are your heroes? Why?

- What do you really want to do with your life? Are you doing it now?

- What would you change if you could?

- Make a list of the top five priorities in your life. Do you give them priority?

- What is the worst thing that has ever happened to you?

- What do you consider your greatest accomplishment?

- What brings you the greatest joy?

- Do the people you love know it? Are you sure? How can you be sure?

I wrote the answers to these questions in my journal. I soon realized I wanted far more out of my life than I was getting. I needed to make a lot of changes.

3. Make a list of the things you need to change. When someone wants to get stronger physically they must stop certain things, like eating junk food and start other things like eating healthy and exercising. The same process has to happen with emotional fitness. There are things to stop doing and things to start doing.

4. Make a list of things you want to start doing. I decided to go back to college. I needed to know how to be on my own. There was a lot to learn and I was behind. I also wanted to start having some fun in my life. Things that *I* thought were fun, not my kid's or someone else's idea of fun, but mine.

A. I decided I would look the best I can at my current age instead of trying to look like I did at twenty-five, (which by the way is a ridiculous standard to even try to attain). But being the best I can be at my current age is doable. What that meant for me was:

1. Taking care of my body, by eating right and reducing stress. Also, to always be in some type of exercise program. I wanted to find a healthy weight for myself and then vow to keep my weight within

five pounds of that ideal weight; not losing more than five, nor gaining more than five. This would keep me from getting so far out of shape that I would not want to even try to get back into shape. I have found that eating a lean protein, low carbohydrate diet along with fresh healthy vegetables daily, has enabled me to keep my five pound vow.

2. Another way to look great at my current age is taking care of my skin. Since then, I have stayed out of the sun for the most part, using bronzers and sunless tanners if I felt I needed to look tanned. Sun is the number one enemy of beautiful youthful skin. I cleanse and moisturize every morning and every night, regardless of how tired I am. *Consistency is imperative for youthful skin and time will reveal the dedication to this daily discipline.*

3. Giving the illusion of youth has several elements; one is a positive attitude and a determination to staying young. Another is staying current in makeup and clothing styles. A very lovely older lady once told me to always buy 4 fashion magazines a year, to make sure I was up on new styles and makeup techniques. I have found this to be very helpful. I buy one at the start of each new season every year.

4. One final rule in being the best at my current

age is to celebrate the things I like about myself and play those up, and stop obsessing about the flaws that I must live with. I am much more realistic---because aiming for a perfect body is exhausting. My goal is; *the best at my current age,* just as long as it is truly *my best.* I cannot measure myself by what others may or may not look like at this age. To be extraordinary is kicking it up a few notches, never get into the habit of saying, "well I am better than…" and use an example of someone who is less than extraordinary.

B. I also decided to broaden my base of friends. Friendships are a necessity for the long haul of life itself. I discovered I needed about five or six very loyal, trustworthy friends to aid me on the journey. I had only two when I began the pursuit of extraordinary living a few years ago. I now have numerous acquaintances that **care** a little and few friends who **care** a lot. I say without hesitation the relationship I have with these few is definitely divine. I prayed for God to send me kindred spirits who would love me through everything, and He did. I needed friends who would not only cry with me when things were bad, but who could actually celebrate with me when things were wonderful! Things like back stabbing, jealousy and gossip, in a friendship can hurt more deeply than a physical wound. You will make friends in life. I advise asking God to help you find them. He chooses perfectly.

5. Get to know God intimately. I knew *about* God all of my life. But when life got hard, I got to know God. Knowing about Him is not enough in the dark hours of the night. There will be times when there is no one, not even the closest of friends, who can relieve the deep pain you are experiencing, who can give you hope when there is none in sight, who can bring peace and comfort to you aching heart. God and He alone has the power to do all of this and more. He has made me sing and dance in the darkest of nights. He has never left me alone on this journey and I know that He will not let you down if you take the time to get to know God intimately.

Overcoming Fear

"One night during a thunderstorm, a mother was tucking her young son into bed. She was about to turn the light off when he asked in a trembling voice, 'Mommy, will you stay with me all night?' The mother gave him a warm reassuring hug and said tenderly, 'I can't, Dear. I have to sleep in Daddy's room.' After a brief pause, the boy replied, 'The big sissy!'"

Fear. It is such a small word, yet it's four letters carry a power so intense that it can grip and paralyze each of it's victims. The anxiety it produces is a monster that lurks just beneath the surface of our lives. "Anxiety's one creative facet is that it feeds on itself. Legitimate concerns can turn into worry. Worry becomes anxiety and anxiety can dominate life." Anxiety just causes us to sit, stew and stress out, all the while robbing us of joy and peace that we must have to live an extraordinary life. As a prisoner of fear we will be completely miserable, unable to live life with any signs of joy or hope. During these fearful times thoughts like: "You are all alone...God can't handle this problem," or "God could care less about your crisis," come to us causing us to doubt God's love and involvement in our lives. God is able and we must have faith that He is big enough to handle any problem - *our* problem. Our mistake is to focus on the hopeless circumstances instead of on God's power to help! *"See, the Sovereign Lord comes with power, and his arm rules for him...He tends his flock like a shepherd: He gathers the lambs in his arms and **carries them close to his heart;** he gently leads."* (Isaiah 40:10-11 emphasis added) I know this as reality. I have felt Him carry me close to His heart.

Complete Trust

The only power over fear is complete trust and rest in God. Have you noticed that it is impossible to trust and worry at the same time? The usual pattern is to volley back and forth between the two at first and then give in to one of them.

When I was a little girl in Oklahoma we had tornado season every spring. It was on one of those cool, quiet May evenings that I was to learn an important lesson in trust.

Our family was sitting at home this particular night. Daddy was reading, my big brother Larry was busy working on a model airplane, while I colored a glorious picture of springtime flowers. Mom was busy getting my baby sissy, Debbie ready for bed, when suddenly, without any warning, the wind and rain started pounding against the big picture window in our living room. Within moments my mom and daddy had tuned into the local radio station for a weather report. With concerned brow my mom began to gather up blankets, coats and my baby sister. Soon our phone began to ring from concerned neighbors nearby urging my dad to open up the church basement for shelter. The basement was the neighborhood storm cellar. Everyone—sinner and saint—would gather underneath the giant brick church building when a storm came up.

This was a *real* storm—not just a warning! The weatherman said a tornado had been sighted and it was heading straight for our little town of Wewoka. Everyone was urged to seek shelter—fast!

My dad grabbed the keys to the church with my brother right behind him. They were met by others in our yard, all hurrying to the basement. My mom held my baby sister tightly as she threw a blanket snugly over her. She headed out the door of our home. As the wind grabbed at her on the porch, I heard my instructions. "Wait here until daddy comes back for you; the wind is too strong."

There I stood, alone, in the middle of the deserted house, eagerly waiting for the sight of my daddy to take me to safety. Soon, the tall familiar figure that I knew and trusted, stood in the doorway. He had come to take me to safety. My dad took me by the hand and said gently, "Pamala do not let go of my hand, okay?" He didn't have to worry. I wasn't about to let go. I'm sure the perspiration on my sweaty little hands had instantly turned to super glue.

As we stepped outside into the darkest of night, I could feel the hard rain beating down upon me. The wind was fierce, tearing at my coat. Then we heard it! It was the deafening sound of a tornado. I could see it's gray funnel winding up toward the sky as it headed straight toward us!

"Hold on Pamala. Hold on baby. Daddy knows the way. Just don't let go of my hand." Within moments we were safe inside the old basement. My dad motioned toward an old table. "Pamala, go sit under that old wood table. I want you to stay there until this storm passes over."

It was cold and uncomfortable, not to mention boring under that old wood table. But I knew the storm was tearing things apart just above us, and that my daddy had brought me to a safe place. I had trusted him as we ran through the pouring rain to get here, and even though it was most uncomfortable, I stayed under that table for a long, long time that night. I wasn't really worried; I trusted my dad's wisdom and knowledge of tornadoes. I chose to rest and not be afraid.

Since then I have endured many storms in my life. Some have been emotional, some spiritual, others physical, but all of them have been scary. But through each of them I have learned that if I hold tightly to my faith in God and trust Him to guide me to safety,

I can find rest, even comfort, during the roughest of storms. I can endure and come through in a majestic way, being better because of it, not bitter or fearful.

You will need endurance on your journey to live above and beyond ordinary. I am thankful for the strength I now possess inside - strength of heart, soul, and body. I am blessed to have the help of a few tried and true friends that will love me through whatever comes. I now possess the internal strength that it takes to live a life of extraordinary living, and so can you.

Chapter 2

Persistence

Persistence a requirement in pushing passed a life of ordinary. Webster defines persistence as: **Per-sist-ent adj**. 1. continuing, especially in the face of opposition, etc. 2 continuing to exist or endure 3 constantly repeated – **per-sist-ence n**.

Athletes talk about having mental toughness. All athletes are gifted physically, but only the mentally tough rise to the top. Mental toughness means never watching the scoreboard. It means knowing the game plan and executing the game plan no matter the circumstances. It means playing until last second ticks off the clock. Persistence is the sweat in extraordinary living!

Since we cannot see into the future, we cannot anticipate what is coming next. That's why persistence is the key to accomplishing extraordinary goals, and seeing impossible dreams come true. Without persistence, all you're doing is stopping and starting things throughout your life. Remember the Fitness Gym membership? Or starting a new motivational book, like this one only to lay it aside? Or that degree you have began but not finished? The list is endless right? I will break down the idea of persistence so you can develop this discipline into your life.

Establish accountability

Everybody needs someone they can trust, there needs to be a few people who knows your *whole* story, not just your current crisis. There can be no holding back in these relationships. They must know the worst and the best about you. A true accountability relationship requires that the other person knows the good, bad, and the ugly. Accountability is a team sport. You cannot go it alone. Even the Lone Ranger had Tonto, Batman had Robin, Tinker Bell had Peter Pan; you get the picture.

You might begin by asking your church if they have a mentoring program. Or you may have an older person who has had a profound impact in your life. If they live close by you may chose to meet once a month; if they live a distance away you can use email, telephone calls, and an occasional visit. But the door of communication must always stay open.

Staying Focused

Resist the desire to find a short cut. I'm all for the shortest distance between point A and point B. And I don't want to spend a single day doing a lot of unnecessarily work. But the easy way is seldom the right way. Part of what makes any difficult experience so challenging is all the distractions. There will be obstacles in our path. Distractions abound to break our concentration. Life's little "fires" break out and just the time you have one extinguished, another breaks out. Detours and roadblocks are inevitable in life. But I'll confess it's hard to focus on what you can't see. What we need is to catch a glimpse of God and to stay focused on *"what is unseen. For what is seen is temporary, but what is unseen is eternal"* (2 Cor. 4:18).

Where we look is where we end up going. Our focus, in a large part, determines our future. One more illustration will serve our purpose. When Jesus came walking on the water to His disciples, Peter asked to join Him. Stepping out of the boat and walking on the water was the thrill of a lifetime! But when Peter took his eyes off of Jesus and *"saw the wind, he was afraid and, beginning to sink, cried out, 'Lord, save me!'"* (Matt. 14:30). If our attention is always focused on our weakness, our heartache, our mistakes, we will only experience fear. But when we set before our eyes God's Word, His promises, and His purposes for our life, an assurance will begin to take root and grow in our hearts.

Our attempt to stay focused needs to be addressed in three ways: daily, weekly, and monthly. Some people are content to fly by the seat of their pants, but most of us need some kind of plan or schedule.

1. Plan daily: there are 24 hours, or 1,440 minutes in every day. We need to discover a style of planning that works for us so that we live *on* and *with* purpose. I have always tried to do the most important thing first thing in the day. In other words, first things first. Then I would move on to the next most important thing. Of course plans don't always work out but chances are that you will accomplish more if you have a plan when you begin your day. You may be a list kind of person or you may organize your work from a laptop computer or Palm Pilot. Whatever works best for you is what matters.

2. Evaluate weekly: the temptation is to constantly be correcting our course and, if we're not careful, we will be chasing our tail. Evaluating at the end of a week is a better idea than doing it on an hour-by-hour basis. I encourage you to get out your calendar, make plans, and chart the course for the coming week.

3. Adjust monthly: Just like I go to the chiropractor once a month for a maintenance visit, adjusting our course and plans on a monthly basis is a good idea. I need to evaluate where I have been and attempt to project where I am going. You can't drive looking in the rear view mirror, but there is value in looking back to make sure you are not going in circles.

4. Respect and Deal with Fatigue. Fatigue is a given. It's not a matter of *if*, but *when*. When fatigue sets in we lose our ability to concentrate, and our will to press on is weakened. Fatigue makes cowards of us all! There are three elements to aid us in dealing with fatigue:

• **Rest**: Sleep is something our bodies need to do; it is not an option. An infant averages 14 hours of sleep, the mature adult averages 7 ½ hours, and the senior adult (over seventy-five) averages 6.[1] Children and even adolescents need at least 9 hours of sleep each night to do their best. Even though the exact reasons for sleep remain a mystery, we do know that during sleep many of the body's major organs and regulatory systems continue to work actively. Some parts of the brain actually increase their activity dramatically,

[1] Pierce J. Howard, *The Owner's Manual For The Brain* (Austin, TX: A Bard Press Book, 1994) 92.

and the body produces more of certain hormones. An internal biological clock regulates the timing for sleep. It programs each person to feel sleepy during the nighttime hours and to be active during the daylight hours. Light is the cue that synchronizes the biological clock to the 24-hour cycle of day and night. Sleepiness due to chronic lack of adequate sleep is a big problem in the United States and affects many children as well as adults.

However, studies show that the length of sleep is not what causes us to be refreshed upon awaking. The key factor is the number of complete sleep cycles we enjoy. A sleep cycle lasts an average of 90 minutes; 65 minutes of normal, or non-REM (rapid eye movement) sleep; 20 minutes of REM sleep (in which we dream), and a final 5 minutes of non-REM sleep. "A person who sleeps only 4 cycles (6 hours) will feel more rested than someone who has slept 8 to 10 hours but who has not been allowed to complete any one cycle because of being awakened before it was completed."[2]

Staying up late and getting up earlier than normal are sure ways to leave us fatigued for the day ahead. It's best (if possible) to go to bed at the same time each night and to use the 90 minute cycle and work

---

[2] Ibid, 93.

backwards to determine the time you should go to bed to wake refreshed.

• **Exercise**: When we talk about exercise we need to note that there is a difference between fitness and health. Many people think of strenuous exercise as the only way to health and fitness. When in fact, there's a well established and growing body of knowledge that shows mild to moderate physical activity is the best way to health. You don't have to become a gym rat to get the exercise that you need.

Books and magazines abound on the topic of exercise, but most agree that an elevated heart rate due to walking or bike riding for 30 minutes 3 times a week will be adequate. Regular exercise assists in three crucial areas. First, it will improve stamina. And stamina is essential to persistence. Second, it enhances flexibility. This is both true in the physical and emotional sense of the word. Third, exercise improves the quality of life. It reduces stress; it lifts moods, and helps you sleep better.

The top active living tips include simple things like:
    a. Use the stairs instead of the escalator or lift at work.

    b. Park your car in the parking bay furthest from

the supermarket.

c. Don't use the remote control to change TV channels; get up and do it manually. A sedentary lifestyle only contributes to our desert experience. Resist the temptation to simply do nothing.

"Nothing in this world can take the place of persistence. Talent will not; nothing is more common than unsuccessful men with talent. Genius will not; unrewarded genius is almost a proverb. Education will not; the world is full of educated derelicts. Persistence and determination alone are omnipotent. The slogan 'press on' has solved and always will solve the problems of the human race."[3]

No doubt you have heard this story but it is worth repeating for obvious reasons. The value of courage, persistence, and perseverance has rarely been illustrated more convincingly than in the life story of this man

Failed in business age 22

Ran for Legislature--defeated age 23

Again failed in business age 24

Elected to Legislature age 25

Sweetheart died age 26

---

3 Calvin Coolidge in *Bits and Pieces.*

Had a nervous breakdown age 27

Defeated for Speaker age 29

Defeated for Elector age 31

Defeated for Congress age 34

Elected to Congress age 37

Defeated for Congress age 39

Defeated for Senate age 46

Defeated for Vice President age 47

Defeated for Senate age 49

Elected President of the United States age 51

That's the record of Abraham Lincoln.[4]

The whole of idea of persistence is staying with it, never quitting no matter what. Your dreams may take a lifetime to accomplish, but you have a lifetime to see it through, regardless of how long or short that lifetime may be. When you get to the end of it, what you did persistently will show up in your life. What will it look like if you continue the course you are taking right now?

Be persistant in the following and at the end of your days here on earth, you will have lived <u>extraordinary.</u>

4 *Bits and Pieces,* July 1989.

1. Commit to your dreams

2. Listen to wise, successful people

3. Set deadlines

4. Follow through

5. Make the most of your day, get up early

6. Have fun even if it is work

7. Help others succeed

8. Keep a great attitude

9. Set goals, achieve them

Chapter 3

Living Through Extraordinary Challenges

Did I do it right?

We had raised our baby girl, our firstborn by the Book. Sunday school and church every Sunday; Youth group on Wednesday night; church camp every summer; the whole nine yards. We prayed before every meal and when we tucked her into bed at night. And to top it off - her daddy was the pastor of the church. But by the time she was in junior high trouble was brewing; and there was no way we could imagine what lay ahead for our daughter.

It started with decisions about the kind of kids she chose to hang around with. Then she began removing the screen off her bedroom window and sneaking out at night. Somehow she managed to graduate from a Christian high school. Soon after her senior year she was determined that she had found the love of her life and announced her plans to be married, but just ten days before the wedding she broke off the engagement.

When things can't get any worse

Still reeling for the events from the past months she came in sheepishly one evening and asked if she could speak with us. And then she spoke those four words every parent dreads to hear from an unwed daughter: "Mom, Dad, I'm pregnant." One year to the date that she canceled the wedding; little baby Chelsea Pamala was born. The next four years she found her escape in drugs and alcohol and poor choices in men. Once more she announced a baby was on its way with an absentee father. A few months later Jewel Katelyn was born prematurely and spent the next two months in the neonatal unit. She barely weighed 3 pounds at birth, and had a nutritional deficit from the very beginning. Jewel needed to be kept in the Intensive Care Neonatal Unit for six full weeks. The trauma of Jewels condition once again caused our daughter Apryl to revert back to her troubled lifestyle, leaving me with her two children. We made room for Chelsea and prepared the bassinet for baby Jewel. I had become a full-time mom of a preschooler and infant once again, this time at age 42. We settled in for an uncertain future.

Coming Home

We prepared the guest list, bought the food and I

decorated our house to the rafters. Our friends came and cars lined both sides of the street for a block in both directions. We sang carols, shared stories, and told favorite family memories. And that's when the doorbell rang.

"Who could that be?" I wondered. Maybe somebody's car was blocking a neighbor's driveway. I opened the door and there Apryl stood. She looked like she hadn't eaten in weeks and she was soaking wet from walking several miles in a cold December drizzling rain to get back home. She said, "Mom, Dad, I want to come home." Of course all eyes were on this scene at the front door. Most of our friends knew the story of our daughter Apryl. They are the ones who had prayed with us and for Apryl over the years..

We excused ourselves and asked Apryl to come up stairs to speak with us privately. While she was drying off we asked Apryl to explain what she meant when she said, "I want to come home." She made it clear that she was ready for a change of direction in her life. She was ready to do whatever it took to get clean and sober, and—eventually—be a mother to her two daughters.

Apryl asked if she could go down stairs and address the group of 50-60 people. I breathed a breath of hope for the first time in a long time. As we descended the stairs you could have heard a pin drop. In genuine humility Apryl asked for people to forgive her for her destructive lifestyle. She assured them and us that she had asked God for His forgiveness. And that's when the party really began!

We knew there was hard work ahead, but at least we had a start. Within two days Apryl had been accepted into a six month live-in facility known as The House of Grace. At The House of Grace Apryl began to be restored. She learned the importance of trust and loyalty. She learned the value of respecting authority and respecting herself. She studied the Bible every day, and she learned from the other women who lived with her. Most importantly, she learned to experience the grace of God. After a few months Chelsea was able to move in and live with her Mom; and soon after that baby Jewel joined them. Apryl finally had her babies with her. It was here they became a family for the first time.

Apryl has been clean and sober for 11 years at this writing and for the past several years has worked as a drug and alcohol counselor sharing her story and helping others recover from their destructive behavior. God's grace, support from family and friends, and a lot of hard work on Apryl's part is the reason she can use her mistakes to help others through theirs.

Choosing to not act in an ordinary way

Everybody has or will have times of extreme pain or a crisis of some kind; I call it a desert experience. What matters is how we respond to our deserts and how we prepare for the future. In this book I want to encourage you to dance through these tough times. To dance, according to Webster's dictionary is; "to leap or jump about, to move rhythmically in a series of motions or steps". We all move through difficulties in various ways, There is the choice to go trudging or plodding along day after day as a vagabond in the desert, or another way to get through desert experiences is to dance; skipping and leaping! Me - I chose to dance, because it is not ordinary, choosing to dance is an extraordinary way to respond. I have shared this particular story because this experience, along with several others, allows me to speak from experience; validates my advice on the subject of dancing in spite of brutally tough times in life.

Yes, dancing is a choice.

Remember standing on the side of the gym in High School, waiting to be asked to dance, or asking someone to dance with you? It was the moment of decision; would you take the risk and dare to dance?

The music was playing; it looked like it could be fun. What would your decision be? To dance, or stand on the sidelines looking on? Each day is a new opportunity to decide to dance, or not. We all face difficult situations in our lives. What we decide to do in the midst of these difficulties will determine our quality of life. We can stand still and do nothing, thus allowing these hard situations to paralyze us, or we can take action and not allow them to rob us of living life to its fullest, even in the desert.

The dance steps suggested throughout this book are for you to practice and do. I recommend a journal to keep track of your progress. Take your dance lessons seriously and you will learn to dance in the midst of these hard times!

Chapter 4

It Takes Admitting Stuff To Live Extraordinary

Admitting to any weakness is not easy, because once we own up to a revealed truth we are then faced with doing something about it. People who choose to live an extraordinary life will have to learn the lost art of being brutally honest with themselves and admit some "stuff". The very first step to learn in surviving your time in the desert and then finding your way out is **to admit the truth of your circumstance.** Denial will only keep you in a *recurring position of desolation.* Stop what you are doing right now and check the scenery surrounding your life. Could you be living through a desert experience right now? How long has it been since you were in a real desert? I mean the hot, dry, desolate, sand kind of desert! In case it's been awhile let me remind you of what a desert is:

A desert is an area where little or no life exists because of a lack of water. The lack of water and intense heat or cold makes this biome impossible to most life forms.

Temperatures are often extreme. Most of the plants you will see in the desert are species of cactus. Only a few animals, mainly reptile, are well adapted to the hot desert. There are many dangers in the desert; Valley Fever, tick fever, heat/sun stroke, snakes, wild pigs, and coyotes. Disturbances are common in the form of occasional fires or cold weather. Sudden, infrequent, but intense rains cause flooding. Storms emerge abruptly with little protection. All of these making survival in a desert very uncertain. [5]

So, what do you see happening in your life right now? Are you **dry** in your zeal for life itself? Do you **lack the lushness** of fresh dreams and goals? Do secret insecurities and **fears** paralyze you from moving forward? Are you **frequently tired**, with low energy? How long since you acknowledged **anything of beauty** in your life? Has a sudden and **unplanned catastrophe** stolen your joy?

If you answered yes to any of these questions you are very likely in a desert experience of some nature. Why is it so difficult to admit our problems, our needs, our weaknesses, and – yes – even our shortcomings? Coming to terms with the truth about

[5] Available at www.infosearch.com

our circumstances is always the most difficult step in the process of finding the way out of them.

To live above ordinary you must be willing to embrace reality. An illness cannot be treated until it is correctly diagnosed. If left unattended, the illness will only worsen. The same can be said regarding our desert experiences. If ignored or denied, they will take us deeper into the desert. I know this is true based on a past desert experience in my own life.

A few year ago I lost something huge; **a life** I had before my former husband was diagnosed to be terminally ill. I did not lose it on purpose and it wasn't my fault that I lost it; nevertheless, it was gone. I was living a life that I knew and was comfortable with and then suddenly – one day – it was gone. I am not saying that life was perfect, in fact there were many things about it that was a mess, but it was the life I knew and was comfortable with, and I lost it almost overnight!

That life

He and I had served in pastoral ministry for twenty years when the symptoms first began. The search for answers was like the proverbial needle in a haystack. He was poked, prodded, and scanned. Finally he was admitted as a patient at the Medical Center at the University of California at San Francisco. He was patient #345-34-58-6. A team of experts in their memory clinic worked him over the next few months in an attempt to give us an accurate diagnosis. Finally the day came for us to get the test results. We barely spoke a word on our drive to San Francisco. We took our seats and waited for our names to be called. The diagnosis delivered to us by Dr. James Mastrianni that he was suffering from the early stages of **frontal temporal dementia** rocked our world. He had just arrived at a place in his ministry where he thought he would spend many years; perhaps the rest of his ministry. Within a year he had to resign and we moved our family to Oklahoma so that we could survive financially on his disability income.

The move was all but comfortable, new people, new climate, new way of living altogether. Stress was taken to a new level for me, I was now completely in charge of everything for our family, plus deal with a dying man with very little support. I had to make ends meet on a tight budget and pay out of pocket for his care; he needed specialists, and expensive medications.

But it wasn't just about money and position; it was about our identity as a family. I had been a "pastor's wife" for more than twenty years and our children had been the "pastor's children of a very influential church since birth." Our lives had been moved off its foundation. In our new place of residence in Oklahoma, we were just that – residents. No one knew who we were, or cared for that matter. We were just another family relocating from the fascinating Silicon Valley of California to the comfortable, non assuming, little city of Owasso, Oklahoma.

Lost and found

But regardless of how great the loss, we discovered God is still in control. I was reminded of this on a recent boating trip when my friend Jean lost a valuable diamond from her wedding ring. We were off the coast of Florida boating, swimming and snorkeling when she discovered her diamond was missing! She remembered the diamond was intact that morning, so we knew it was lost sometime while we were out on the water. We all combed the boat high and low, but no diamond. So she rested in the fact that it lay somewhere at the bottom of the ocean floor, lost forever! However, when we were about to turn the boat in at the end of the day, Jean looked down and saw the sparkling diamond lying all alone on the boat deck.

The diamond was not lost forever as it certainly appeared to all of us; God knew it's location at all times. None of us understood how we could have missed it the first, second or third time we searched the boat, but we did. That none of us could see it did not matter, it was there all along. It took that last look from the one who missed it the most to see that is was there within reach.

Our losses in life may appear lost forever, never to be seen or heard of again. A career, a spouse, a wayward child, health, money, or dreams unfulfilled. Yet God knows where those losses are and how they came about. He sees them and knows how to restore them back to us. Jean's diamond was insured and she had determined if she could not find her diamond, she would pay a deductible and get a new one, either way she was at peace.

God's plan to restore your loss may be to give you a brand new life or dream. Or He may choose to keep the lost original one safe in His care until the perfect time to reveal its location. Either way we can have absolute confidence that God has it all in His sight at all times and His choice will be the very best one.

So, when facing times of loss; whether you have one now or in the future, you can give it to God, trusting Him to restore it or give you a brand new one of His choosing. But the first step is to honestly admit you are in a desert and want to get out. I have listed below some symptoms that might help you recognize and admit if you are truly experiencing a loss of some kind which has you in a desert right now.

Deserts tend to be:

1. dangerously lonely

2. emotionally draining

3. brutally hard to deal with

4. so diverse that you imagined no one else could possibly relate

5. overwhelmed with sadness;

6. swallowed up by deep darkness

7. abandoned in horrible circumstances

8. One element that seems to hold true in each desert is, regardless of the actual time involved, they all seem painfully long, like they will never end.

Now, someone choosing to live life in an extraordinary way will decide at this point in this book to check out their surroundings, and admit truth to some "stuff", then work on not just staying there, but getting out and moving on. There are deserts like: injustices, disease, violence, hatred and every evil imaginable. Living as a citizen of planet earth, many of these tribulations will come to each of us without warning and it seems for no good reason. These are the source of nearly every "Why?" ever asked.

Deal With Stuff

You can deal with stuff now, or deal with stuff later; but stuff must be dealt with. Some people want to put off today what can be dealt with tomorrow, but tomorrow eventually does come. It is a waste of time dreading certain conversations, decisions or actions which must take place. It is best to face them as soon as possible. Nike's "just do it" philosophy is the appropriate way to face any dreaded task. I have observed that accurate self-assessment is a difficult thing. Sometimes we need the intervention of others. It can be a trusted friend, a mentor, or counselor, but we desperately need objectivity. When in the deepest of deserts we can overlook things that are right in front of us, like the desert itself! Being lost in the middle of a desert is sort of like being injured and needing to be taken to the Emergency Room! Taking the first step to admit where you are, may take some assistance. You may be so ill, disoriented or lost, that you actually need someone else to call 911 for you.

Mustering the courage to ask for help can be a difficult thing. But I can assure you of one thing; once you do, you will wonder why you waited so long. Ours is a culture where asking for help is portrayed as weakness. And in our stubborn refusal to ask for help we can crash and burn. But do not let pride keep you from getting help. Find someone to talk over your situation with and aid you evaluating the terrain around you. Perhaps in talking things over the severity of your experience will become clearer. It may be something very serious, or just something annoying, but find someone to talk with about it. Once you discover the answer, do something about what you can and give the rest to God. You must decide to get over it and move forward in life if it is ever going to be extraordinary.

Do not give into whining

I was reminded recently that if I looked around at the hard circumstances of others I just might decide to choose the life I have. Like the story of the man who was complaining to God about the cross he was called to carry here on earth. God asked him if he wanted to choose another. The man was thrilled at the opportunity to exchange his wearisome cross for another easier one. He gladly turned in his cross to God, then is shown to the "cross room" to choose another. After looking around the room at the enormous, hideous looking crosses, he sees a tiny one leaning against the wall. He asks God, "Can I have the one over there, against the wall?" God says, "Well sure, but it's the one you just returned to me."

Are you working through some hard circumstance right now and need a better attitude? Always remember someone else has gone through similar before and more than likely far worse.

Time to admit

Without admission there is only bondage. There is strong teaching in the Bible about admission as Jesus Himself said, *"You will know the truth and the truth will set you free"* (John 8:32). Do you want to be free? Free from shame or guilt? Free from blaming yourself? Free from feeling like you can never measure up? Free from the daily trudging through a dry, dead life? Free from feeling like you have danced your last dance? Then get real and ready to admit the truth about your life, because admission is the very first step in learning how to live honestly, and that is an extraordinary choice.

Chapter 5

Keep Going ....
Step Two: Assessment

Once we have come to terms with the fact that we are indeed in a desert we are ready to take the next step. Step Two is assessment. But I'll caution you this step can be overwhelming. Let me explain. Living in denial provides a sense of security – albeit a false sense of security. But once we have admitted the truth of our circumstance the assessment can be like peeling off the layers of an onion.

Damage control

May and June are tornado months in Oklahoma. Nobody wants to believe that a tornado can or will touch down in their neighborhood. But the damaging winds and the sounds of an approaching freight train tell you have been the victims of a twister. When it is safe to go outside or at first light people emerge to assess the damage. Insurance adjusters are soon on the scene to put dollar amounts to the havoc that has been wreaked. And the sights can be overwhelming. Power lines are down; trees uprooted; vehicles picked up and transported, and houses and buildings damaged. It is this kind of closer examination that can cause you to see that things are often worse than you imagined. It can made you want to crawl back into bed and pull the covers over your head.

But things will never get better until we get to the bottom of the damage. It's only when we finally see the depth and breadth of a matter are we able to address it with courage and confidence. We cannot begin to rebuild until a thorough, accurate assessment has been conducted. To assess means, "To evaluate; to make a judgment about." Assessment calls us to investigate and ask the question: "How did I end up in this place in the first place?"

My Own Choices

I believe my most frustrating desert journeys are a result of my own poor choices. Knowing I cannot point a finger at anyone else, that I alone am to blame somehow makes these places more heartbreaking. Assessment forces me to wonder, "If only I had done this differently; if only I had gone about that differently". In looking back I ask myself, "What was I thinking?" Admitting, "Oh yes, I wasn't thinking!"

We see the signs that say, "Desert ahead! No water for many miles! No rest stops for many weeks, perhaps years!" And we still foolishly ignore these signs and defiantly strike out on a journey we insist on taking. We try to fool our self into thinking that all of this sand is a beach, but it ends up being no beach at all. This mirage was actually a hot, dry, lonely, sandy desert. We end up on this self inflicted desert journey because we ignored the signs right in front of us; this is no beach...dah! There is no water or plush resort with room service. I will share one of my own painful choices which landed me in the desert of debt, perhaps you can relate.

I was in my mid-twenties and the opportunity presented itself for me to have a custom home built by a contractor in our church. There was nothing wrong with the house I had – except I thought it was too small. The contractor did a beautiful job. It ended up being more beautiful than I had imagined... and costing more than I could afford! I saw what I wanted and wanted what I saw. Nothing else seemed to matter. I told myself I deserved this house, it was my turn. But when the new mortgage kicked in, the money began to run out. I ended up barely able to pay bills, certainly no extra money for other things, like fun. Sitting around week after week with nothing to do but look at our beautiful house soon began to be a huge bore. My ends began not to meet, if you know what I mean, and then life got really stressful. Soon I was left with no alternative but to sell my home. Looking back I should have thought it through better, counted the cost more intelligently. Instead I fed the craving for more, bigger, newer, regardless how much it would cost in the end. I made a choice that would put me in financial bondage for quite some time.

We all have made decisions our lives that we wished we could do over. We ponder how things could have been different. We long and pray for another chance to do it better next time, a second chance so to speak. If and when given opportunities to do things over, we must stop and realistically count the cost and view things as they really are, make them count; for rarely do we get a third try at it.

In the Bible in the book of Luke Jesus talked about the importance of counting the cost before beginning a project. *"Is there anyone here who, planning to build a new house, doesn't first sit down and figure the cost so you'll know if you can complete it?"* (14:28). Jesus cautioned that failing to count the cost can lead to embarrassment, or worse yet, a desert experience. This is really where our problem of "if I had only" could be remedied many times. Just stop and count the cost; think everything through. Use wisdom, and not be in a hurry. Solomon, the wisest man to ever live said, *"Fools think they need no advice, but the wise listen to others"* (Prov. 12:15 NLT). When investing money, considering marriage, choosing a career, dealing with confrontations, or other decisions, we must take our time. If we slow down and wisely consider a matter from every human perspective, many painful experiences could quite possibly be avoided altogether.

Why do we rush into serious matters without weighing everything wisely? Is it perhaps our own selfish nature? The inner craving to have this desire, this need met at this instant? A sure way of living with fewer regrets is to simply wait. The temptation to act impulsively can add time onto your stay in the desert. So the next time you are making life-changing decisions, may I suggest first you:

1. Consider consequences of past mistakes

2. Look at the end results of this decision; think them through

3. Seek good counsel from a wise person

4. Pray about it and be at peace before proceeding

5. Do not make an emotional decision, these are costly

6. Do not compromise yourself, or your desire to life an extraordinary life

7. Do not choose good when you could wait for great, for good is the enemy of great

Once you feel your decision complies with the above, then you can proceed with confidence that you have done everything in your power to assure that this is the best decision you can make. Move forward boldly and confidently knowing that you can live at peace with your decision come what may.

Choices of Others

If desert experiences were always of our own doing we wouldn't have to look very far to find the source of trouble. But there are times when our desert comes at the hand of somebody else. A drunk driver crosses the highway and injures or kills a loved one; someone looking for a quick buck robs a convenience store and you just happen to be in the wrong place and the wrong time. A trusted family member sexually abuses you without any consequence to them. A father loses his job, stops by the pub on the way home and then vents his furry on his family; your son or daughter chooses a life of addiction to drugs and alcohol taking you down a long road of pain and sorrow with them. This list could go on and on.

Almost everybody I know has been hurt by somebody else. But not everybody will admit it. Some pretend it never happened; others even blame themselves for the bad behavior of the responsible party. They remain victims when God's plan is for them to live a life of happiness and freedom. To attain this please understand you will have to admit the truth, perhaps revealing things that may be costly or somewhat humiliating. But it will be a necessary step to begin to redeem the painful experiences that come your way from the hands of others.

Here are some questions to help you evaluate your status:

1. Have I really identified the source of my pain? Has it come at the hand of somebody else? Or w a s it my bad choices which led me here?

2. Have I blamed myself – to the point of thinking that I deserve what somebody else has done to me?

3. Have I kept quiet – to my own hurt – so that I can protect somebody else?

4. Do I quietly play the role of a victim?

While it's impossible for me to know your particular situation I invite you to consider the following questions for a simple Step Two assessment on a scale of 1 to 5 (with 1 being low and 5 being high)

1. I am experiencing peace in my life on a regular basis   1 2 3 4 5

2. I sense a freedom in my spirit from past failures
                                                            1 2 3 4 5

3. Most days I feel a sense of purpose for my life
                                                            1 2 3 4 5

4. I am rarely depressed or hopeless   1 2 3 4 5

5. I sense God's presence regularly in my life
                                                            1 2 3 4 5

6. I feel hopeful about my future   1 2 3 4 5

7. I can see the bigger picture even in my desert
                                                            1 2 3 4 5

8. I feel as though God has not let me down in my time of need   1 2 3 4 5

9. I am running low on endurance   1 2 3 4 5

10. I know God will see me through this
                                                            1 2 3 4 5

While not meant to be a comprehensive evaluation we can check our position with an honest assessment. You may even want to evaluate your answers with a trusted friend. If your score is low, it is evident that you lack God's peace at this time in your life. God wants to impart His peace, *"And the peace of God, which transcends all understanding, will guard your hearts and minds in Christ Jesus"* (Phil. 4:7). God's peace is there for the asking. Look around you today; what do you see? Do you see nothing but desert stretching out before you as far as the eye can see? Do you see an oasis on the horizon? Can you see the boarder of your desert approaching? Refuse the temptation to take a shortcut. Secure the help of another person if need be, whatever way you choose to discover the truth of your circumstance it must be an honest assessment of how you ended up here.

Chapter 6

Prayer; The Key To An Extraordinary Powerful Life

The practice of prayer and journaling has been my greatest tool throughout my journey to living an extraordinary life. I will complete my twenty-fifth year of journaling at the end of this year. Praying and the practice of journaling have kept me going when nothing else had the power to do so. I have been acquainted with "church" my entire life. My dad was a Baptist pastor and I learned early in life how to follow all the rules expected of a faithful churchgoer – one of which is prayer. However, twenty-four years ago I had an experience that changed my perspective on prayer. I had the idea that prayer was spending about five or maybe even ten minutes of giving God my list of things I wanted Him to do for me. I was wrong. Prayer is so much more than that. *Prayer is the awesome privilege we mortals have to talk with the most powerful Force in the universe – God, Himself – and to hear back from Him.* As I took hold of this truth my approach to prayer radically changed.

Here's how the change took place

Though I had been involved in church my entire life, could teach a Sunday school class, play the piano on Sundays for worship, direct the choir, plan a great church social, lead a Bible study, and tell a person how to become a Christian, there was something missing. I knew everything about working hard for God. I figured I knew Him as well as anyone else – after all, I had spent my life doing stuff for Him. But my intimacy with God was challenged when a new Christian's pure faith was expressed openly one Sunday evening.

Her name was Cheryl and the experience she share with a small group of us left me with many questions. She said nine months earlier in her prayer time God had revealed to her information about her husband's job situation. God had told her that there was going to be a change in his career. He told her the exact time and specifics about an increase in pay. Cheryl said in exactly nine months what God had told her came true. She was excited and awed with the truth of God's word. As I sat there listening to her story I was perplexed. "Why her and not me, Lord? After all, she has only known You for a year – maybe two – and I have been working hard for you for many years. Why would You talk to her so intimately, like a friend, and not me, too?" I needed to have this question answered. So the next morning, after getting the kids off to school, I got my Bible and got on my knees to pray.

I must say that this prayer was different than any of my previous prayers. I had no list to give God that day. I only had one question that I wanted answered. I did not approach Him in reverent formality. I just opened up my Bible and said very directly, "God, I want all of You that is mine to have. I have done everything I thought You wanted me to do. Now I just want You. I want Your presence; I want to have a real conversation with you. I have no idea if You actually communicate with us now like you did in the Bible, but if You do; I want to know how to do it. I want to know if You tell us things like Cheryl said - things about the future that only You know about. Do You still do that?" Then I laid my head down on the Bible asking God to please answer me.

I waited there listening; really expecting an answer. As I waited I heard within my spirit a quiet voice tell me to begin reading my Bible. I opened it and started reading where I had left off a few days earlier. It was Isaiah 42:8 – *"I am the Lord; that is my name! I will not give my glory or my praise to idols. See, the former things have taken place, and new things I declare; before they spring into being I announce them to you."* First of all He wanted me to know that it was Him talking to me. The text began, "I am the Lord!" And then He answered my question: ***yes, He does declare things before they happen!*** That day I know God spoke directly to me. I came to Him in faith, expecting Him to answer, and He did.

The great news is that God desires to communicate with everyone. We do not always need to know about the future, but at times we do. These types of answers to prayer build our faith and cause us to prayer more expectantly. Many time we need to know what is up ahead so our hearts and our lives will be prepared. Jesus told his disciples on a regular basis that he was going to die and three days later He would come back to life again (Mark 10:33, 34). He tried to prepare them and give them hope in the midst of what would seem hopeless circumstances.

We can come to God with questions about anything. The answers do not always come quickly. Sometimes we must keep praying in faith and with persistence. God's answer to your request could be "Yes". Or it could be "No; I have a *better* plan, a *different* plan." But in time there will always be an answer. I challenge you to make time to talk to God and then wait for Him to speak to you. He can choose to do this in many ways, and I assure you He will find a way to communicate with you and I if we just take the time to listen. I say this with every once of confidence that is in me, God does want to communicate with you and I, He desires this kind of intimate relationship with each of us. He offers an extraordinary relationship to us, if we will just take the time to pursue it.

Praying to Accomplish God's Will

Loren Cunningham began Youth With A Mission (YWAM) through an outright supernatural encounter with God. Loren's vision has materialized into a worldwide ministry that has sent out more than 15,000 workers each year helping people in more than 200 different countries. My daughter Amy, at the age of 14, asked God to provide her the money she needed for a summer mission trip. He gave her exactly what she needed through a summer babysitting job. God calls to the young as well as the older, more mature believer. They all hear a call from God to reach out to others in His name. He is available to everyone equally.

Your question may be "How can I know if I am asking according to God's will?" Good question. In his book, *Is That Really You, God?* Loren Cunningham makes these suggestions when seeking to know God's will:

- Submit to His lordship; silence your own thoughts, desires and the opinions of others.

- Allow God to speak to you in the way He chooses. Do not try to dictate to Him concerning methods.

- The methods He commonly uses are: the Bible, the inner voice, circumstances and peace while praying.

- Obey the last thing He told you before moving forward.

- Do not talk about what God said to you until He gives you permission to do so. This is to avoid pride, presumption, and confusion to others who are not ready to receive what God has said to you.

- Be aware of counterfeits like Ouija boards, séances, fortune telling and astrology. The guidance from God will lead you closer to Jesus and true freedom. Other forms will lead you away from God and into bondage.

- Remember, relationship is the most important
  ᶠᵒʳ hearing the voice of God. True
  closer to the guide.[6]

of Intercession

ion literally means "to come
.e in prayer is to stand between
erson. This type of prayer is
ᴵt God places within the heart of
vently for another. They stand in
God and that person. Intercession
's need and places it with God and
something about it. The person being
never know you are praying for them.

I havᵌ given this type of prayer burden only twice in my life. At times I have been inconvenienced and grown weary at their lack of response. There are times when I felt such a heaviness in my heart to pray for these individuals that it would wake me up and keep me praying until I felt some reassurance that all was well. This type of praying takes a great amount of discipline and faith. We must we willing to take our hands off and allow God to work as He chooses in their lives. It is an awesome thing to be trusted to pray

6 Loren Cunningham, *Is That Really You, God?* (Grand Rapids: Chosen Books, 1984), 157-158.

Pamala Chestnut
Communication Specialist
Travel Consultant
918-810-6076
pamala777@yahoo.com
www.livingextraordinarytoday.com
www.pamalachestnut.worldventures.biz

for someone in this manner. Listen to these precise instructions: *"I urge, then, first of all, that requests, prayers, intercession and thanksgiving be made for everyone – for kings and all those in authority, that we may live peaceful and quiet lives in all godliness and holiness. This is good, and pleases God our Savior, who wants all men to be saved and to come to the knowledge of the truth."* (1 Timothy 2:1-4)

Prayers for Healing

Does God heal today? Or, an even more relevant question; will God heal me? It is easy to theorize about suffering when you're not doing any. But when it comes knocking at your door, it's a whole new ball game. As Ron Dunn has said, "pain can make us desperate."2 Let me assure you that I believe in healing. I believe that all healing is divine, whether it comes at the hand of a skilled surgeon, prescription drugs, or an intervention of God without the assistance of another person or substance. While there are no guarantees, it is always right to ask God to heal us. For the past year my dad has been fighting lung cancer. It certainly made no sense that he had it, since he had never smoked a day in his life, however he did. I say he did, past tense, because he just received word that he is now cancer free. Yes, at the age of 84, stage 3 cancer God used prayer, faith and natural medicine along with traditional medicine to heal him. He did what he could, then rested in God's healing power to do the rest in his time. My dad had quite a fight, but he never doubted that he would be healed!

We should always pray for ourselves and others to be healed. First, let your request be made known. Ask. Be specific. We are told, *"Do no be anxious about anything, but in everything, by prayer and petition, with thanksgiving, present your requests to God."* (Philippians 4:6) Prayer is a mystery and God invites us into the mix.

Second, we must be willing to submit to the Father's will. Here, again, Jesus leads the way. *"Yet not as I will, but as you will."* (Matthew 26:39) Wanting what God wants more than what I want has always been the toughest for me to get to. I am sure I have looked very much like an overly tired child who needs a nap, but refuses it until finally they, like me, relax and give in out of sheer exhaustion. God knows what is best for me and you, trust Him.

Praying for the impossible

It takes faith to accomplish the impossible. Faith that God is absolutely faithful. *"The Lord is faithful to all of his promises and loving toward all he has made."* (Ps. 145:13) Feelings or perceptions cannot be the basis of faith. If you can see it, then it is not faith. Belief always will proceed accomplishing the impossible in your life. What impossible circumstance or dream do you have to give to God? When we are convinced that anything is possible, we become unstoppable. Take your impossibilities to God and believe that he can take care of them.

Humpty Dumpty walks again

Eight years ago I had a horrendous accident which broke five vertebras and crushed six discs in my neck and lower back. I was told by several specialists that I was "Humpty Dumpty" and could not be put back together again. This is not what I wanted too hear, nor did I believe God wanted me in a wheelchair for the rest of my life. After a long search, I discovered a group of doctors in Northern California who specialized in spinal reconstruction. They took my case believing I was an excellent candidate for the surgery and expected it to be very successful. They informed me it would be about a ten hour surgery and a long recovery.

I was convinced God was directing me to proceed with the surgery even though it would take a lot of effort to set things up in my absence. Our daughter Amy consented to move into our house to look after her brother while I was in California undergoing the surgery. Everything fell into place and I was on my way to California for the surgery.

The morning of the surgery I felt good; confident. The surgeons came in and assured me they were certain all would go well and had scheduled nine holes of gold for later that day. But they never made that tee time.

About half way into the surgery I began to experience loss of blood pressure. My back was opened up and nerves exposed – this was not a good time for things to become complicated. The anesthesiologist began the procedure to bring my pressure up, but with no success. Finally they decided that I must be losing blood from a major organ. This meant they needed to call in a vascular surgeon to go in and "look around." While they were bringing me out of the deep sleep and attempting to *flip me over* for the vascular surgeon, I could hear them talking frantically; almost yelling. The doctors were saying things like, "We're losing her!" "Hurry, she's not responding!" I remember it perfectly. Hysterical thoughts were racing through my mind. I cried to myself, "I'm dying, oh God, who will take care of the girls?" (Referring to my granddaughters Chelsea and Jewel) God said to me, "Pamala, I have them in my hands now and always." With that I was overcome by a great peace and, in fact, I died.

I know I died. I had never read an account of anyone dying. This experience was not a dream – it was real; it was true; it happened to me. I was walking through a very dark tunnel toward an intense light. The light was like a million sparklers, you know, the ones the kids play with on the Fourth of July. I was walking through this dark tunnel into the bright sparkling light. I remember feeling a peace which is beyond any known to me before. There are not sufficient words to begin to describe this peace. I could see I was headed to the doorway of heaven. It was beautiful. I was not afraid, I was filled with joy! Just as I got close to the light I felt a hand on my left shoulder and then I heard a voice say, "Pamala, it is not time for you to go my child." I knew it was the voice of Jesus. He took his hand and gently turned me around and with that done I awoke in the recovery room. I had no idea that several days had passed. At the time I could not speak so I motioned for my friend Tricia to give me something to write with. I was very weak but managed to write, "I died." She looked at me puzzled and said, "You died? You will have to tell me all about that later!"

When I was able to speak I did tell her and other family members about the entire experience. It was about day nine when the doctor came into my room and said, "Pamala, I need to tell you about something that happened during your surgery." I looked at him, smiled and said, "I died, didn't I?" He looked at little upset and asked me who had told me. I got the opportunity to describe the entire experience to him in detail. I know he was perplexed by what I had to say, because there was no way for me to know what had gone on during surgery without someone telling me. I had indeed died and recalled the entire incident; no one could explain otherwise.

Why?

Why did I die, remember it perfectly and come back to this life? Perhaps to tell this story to you or help others at the hospital have a deeper faith in God, or give validity of the afterlife to skeptics. I cannot say for certain, but I do believe God gave this particular experience to me to help others facing an ominous future. I have told it repeatedly to my kids and grandkids when they seen fearful about death. From what I got a glimpse of, there is absolutely nothing to fear if heaven is where you are headed. Heaven is a place of magnificent beauty, euphoric peace, indescribable joy, and is bursting with happiness. I know; I experienced it up close and personal.

Praying for personal desires

I had come to a point in my life that living as a single woman was very lonely. I felt that I was ready to open my heart and wanted to be sure God agreed. So, the following week I called each of my five faith filled praying friends and asked them to fast and pray for God to send me someone to love and be loved by. My own prayer about this went something like this; " God, I do not know if you want to send me a husband yet, or just a safe companion to spend time with, but I cannot bear being alone any longer. I am not asking for him to know as much as I know about the Bible, however he must love you and have a continuing desire to know you more intimately! Also, please let him be a worshipper, like I am. (I then raised my right hand to God as I often do when in worship, and said with almost a p.s.), and make him drop dead gorgeous, amen!" The next day God would indeed take care of this request…perfectly.

It was Labor Day weekend and friends asked me to ride with them on their motorcycles to a Harley

Davidson Grand opening for the 2005 models. I went along, just for fun. While I was looking at some tee shirts I noticed a gorgeous man walk through the door. I watched his behavior throughout the morning to see if he was one of the typical party guys I had met at these types of events numerous times before. He was not, so I decided I needed to meet him. I saw him walk outside knowing he would return to be with his friends, I positioned myself in front of the doorway that he would have to pass back through. As he approached me he was carrying a Mountain Dew in both hands, but stopped in front of me and said with a big smile, "hi". We had small talk for a moment and then I asked him about the So Cal tee shirt he was wearing. "Are you from California, or did you just pick up the shirt somewhere?" He replied, "No, I'm not, I got it at a bike shop here in Tulsa where I bought my chopper.' Then he went on to ask me, "how about that cross you are wearing, it that just a piece of jewelry? Or does it mean something to you?"

I then gave him the full blown testimony of what Jesus meant to me. He stood and listened intently, but when I finished, I then asked him, "how about you? Are you a believer in this cross?" He said, "Oh yeah, Jesus is my savior, but I'm not just a casual believer I am really into it, I am also a worshiper!" At the same time he raised his hand to demonstrate the word worship, just in case I did not follow what he was talking about. As you can imagine I just about fell over, because even though I did not even know this man's name, God had given me a perfect sign that he was sent to me by God himself. I did not know if he was to be a safe companion, or my future husband, but I was certain he was mine for now!

Prayers of Gratefulness

I so enjoy the times my children come to me and tell me they love me and leave without asking for one thing. I love when they call just to say "hi" and say they miss me. Likewise, I am certain God enjoys this kind of love from His kids. Sometimes prayer should just be about gratefulness. Prayer is talking about what is in your heart. Hopefully you express love and adoration for God as well as your need for His care. Take time to say "Thank You." The Bible says in 1 Chronicles 16:8-12 *"Give thanks to the Lord, call on his name; make known among the nations what he has done. Sing to him, sing praise to him; tell of his wonderful acts...let the hearts of those who seek the Lord rejoice...seek his face always...Remember the wonders he has done, his miracles."* Take time to simply say, "I love you, God. Thank You for all of my blessings."

Honest Prayers

There will be times you are confused by what God seems to be doing, or not doing. Tell Him what's on your mind. You can say anything to Him; He is big enough to take it. So go ahead – dish it out. I have certainly had moments of anger questioning why God has allowed suffering and tragedy to come to our family. I do not have the complete answer yet, but I do know He wants others to know a supernatural peace, comfort, strength and joy that is always available, even during lengthy times of suffering. In difficult times it is okay to ask God, "why". Jesus, Himself did when he asked a similar question. *"My God, my God, why have you forsaken me?"* (Matthew 27:46) God never seems offended by anyone asking Him "Why?" He just wants us to talk to Him about what is in our heart. As a mother I know when my children are upset and usually know what it is that has upset them; but I love it when they trust me enough to come and share their questions and their needs. I love it when we can talk about them together. God also wants us to come to Him when we are angry or confused. He has brought comfort to me even if the circumstances did not change. There are times we must trust the fact that He is God and we are not. His ways are higher than ours and we must rest in the knowledge that He is going to work all things for our good in the end.

"Ask and it will be given you; seek and you will find; knock and the door will be opened to you. For everyone who asks receives; he who seeks finds; and to him who knocks, the door will be opened." (Matthew 7:7, 8) This verse is pro-active. Prayer is not passive, but aggressive. The verse implies consistency. We are instructed to keep on asking, seeking and knocking until the answer comes. I know my kids can be relentless when they want me to do something for them. When Amy was young she would tug at my arm until I would stop and listen to her. How wonderful that God is never too busy to listen to us. He loves spending time with us.

In times of aloneness, suffering and sadness, God wants to comfort you and me. To think that He is listening and available 24/7 is beyond my human understanding. I do not know how prayer works; I just know that it does. You do not need magic words, a special formula or access code; simply call out His name. He is listening.

Praying for your family

If you are a mom, then you will need to understand the importance of praying for your children. Pray for their protection and health; daily. Pray that they find Jesus at an early age and fall in love with Him and His word. Pray for wisdom to help them become all that God intended them to be one day. If you will notice I said, "all He intended", not what YOU have in mind for them. This is a hard discipline at times, because our children are an extension of us to a degree. But umbilical cords are cut at birth, from that moment on it is our responsibility to help them become independent and thrive on their own. God never intended children to remain dependant on us for the rest of their lives.

Freeing Amy

My middle child Amy was born quite timid and shy. This sweet little girl loved being as close to me as possible. She hated, even feared my absence. Amy was no trouble, so she was easy to take with me anywhere. I loved her snuggles, and I admit; her adoration of me. She literally hated being away from me. In fact, she was so miserable in pre-school we took her out. But eventually the dreadful day arrived for her to go to kindergarten. I will never forget the scared look on her face, tears on

81

her cheeks and mouthing to me, "mommy, I'm super scared." Seeing her so fearful of my absence soon made me face reality; my daughter was miserable and I needed to help her get over this fear if she was ever to have a peaceful life. From that moment on my desire for her was that she grow into a healthy, independent adult. This new quest was not easy, it meant me pushing her to go and do things out of her comfort zone. It meant me seeing her struggle with failures from time to time. Growing independent meant she needed me less and less which hurt me at times. But, I am thrilled to tell you by the time Amy was fourteen; she boarded a train, alone, in California; made several scheduled and unscheduled changes on her on; arrived in New Mexico to spend the next 3 weeks working on an Indian Reservation; with people she had never met before; to minister in a culture that she had never experienced…all without me tagging along.

Prayers for our children must include prayers for ourselves to be willing to let them go, allowing them to thrive and prosper on their own.

Journaling a Record

A part of my prayer experience is time spent writing in a journal. I don't start with "Dear diary," but it is very much like a diary. Journaling is a record of your thoughts, prayer requests, an account of your daily activities, as well as a record of what God is doing in your life. Without some form of records, valuable proof is missing. Records are indispensable. Birth certificates, marriage licenses, drivers' licenses, death certificates and court proceedings are all valuable records. A journal is similar. I journal for several reasons:

- I want to look back and be reminded of all the wonders in my life.

- It reminds me that I am making progress.

- I get to see answers to my prayers and how long I prayed for someone or something.

- It is also great therapy. I can vent pretty well on paper.

- I am encouraged when I read how God lifted me up on a sad day by bringing a wonderful surprise into my life. I seem to have a bad memory on my own. My journal serves as a reminder of God's goodness.

- It serves as a record of those moments in life you want to always remember.

Journaling can be done anytime. All you need is a paper and pen. Or perhaps you prefer to use your computer. I have all of my journals for the past twenty-four years except one that I left on an airplane last Christmas. I tried for weeks and weeks to find it. I felt like I lost a year of memories.

My first journal was a book of blank pages for me to write whenever I felt like it. Then I started being more accountable using a journal with dates on it. I could see how many days I kept up with my journal and the days I skipped. I now have such a love for this time that I rarely, if ever, miss a day in an entire year. I now prefer to use a journal with a short inspirational message with room provided for me to respond to the message. I have found time after time I needed exactly what was written on that day. It was as if it was written just for me. I know God has used this discipline to guide me, show me His love, answer questions, correct wrong thinking and convict me of sin in my life. I strongly encourage you to get a journal that comes with some type of daily message or challenge. It can help you begin this discipline by giving you something to reflect on and write about.

But the most important thing about journaling is to do it. Journaling will become your record of growth, strength and courage through the good and bad times of your life. There are times I am proud as I read of my steps forward and other times embarrassed at the life I see on the pages of my journal. My life can look a lot like a ship on a raging sea; lost, scared and coming apart at the seams. It's all there for me to reflect on. I am thankful I have both the good and the bad written down. I have found it is during the raging storms of my life I learn the most, change the most and become a stronger, better person.

All the avenues of praying that I have mentioned have changed my life drastically. I also know that because I have prayed for others, their lives have also been changed. Prayer is the most effective tool available to you and I in our pursuit to live extraordinary. We just need to use it.

Chapter 7

Extraordinary Romance

A few years ago my family was visiting in the home of some friends of ours for a day of swimming and sunning and barbecuing. When we had all the water our bodies could stand for one day, we migrated to the bedrooms and bathrooms to change into dry clothing. Every room had been carefully groomed for our visit that day. Every room except the one that I was told to use…the master bedroom. As I opened the door, my eyes fixed upon a horrendous sight. This room bore no resemblance to a bedroom at all, except for a bed against the side wall. As I sought for a place to disrobe, I could not help but see what this room had become. It was one of the most unkempt storage rooms I've ever seen.

To the left was a dresser. It was covered with old newspapers. (If you need a magazine dating back ten years or more, I know where you can find it.) The dresser sagged from the weight of the paper piled two feet on top. The drawers were half opened with clothes sticking out here and there. As my eyes scanned the rest of the room, I noticed a mountainous pile of clothes lying next to an ironing board. It looked like ironing for a family of twenty. (There were only four residing here.) As I continued to scan the room my eyes rested on an old bird cage which the resident had vacated, but the evidence that he had been there was still very obvious. There was a desk with piles of books, several dirty coffee mugs along side a computer dating back to the age of the dinosaurs. There were several mounds of clothing scattered everywhere which looked like the owner had quickly stepped out of them leaving them in perfect little piles all around the room. It was dark, dingy, depressing and actually very dirty.

But the most curious sight of all was the bed itself. Smack in the middle of this queen-size bed, nestled between the sheets, laid a massive German shepherd. This was most certainly his territory - the room reeked with dog odor. I must have set a record that day in speed dressing. I could not get out of that room fast enough. I now viewed my host and hostess in a new light. I noticed they were not courteous to each other. They never touched or exchanged glances of gratitude. In fact, they did not seem even remotely fond of each other. This all added up after having visited their love nest.

The room I just described is probably the only one

of its kind anywhere. But just in case your love nest is being neglected, let's talk about the bedroom.

Sensuous bedding

The sheets should be clean, even if they can't be new. A light powdering can make them fresh and inviting. Scented sheets are not new in creating an enticing bedroom; women of the 14th century sprinkled rose petals on their beds to make them smell wonderfully romantic. Solomon even perfumed his carriages with myrrh and spices. His beloved speaks of wonderful fragrance being spread everywhere, letting many delicious scents flow to allure her lover (Song of Solomon 4:16).

If your budget will allow, invest in satin sheets (even the synthetic ones feel quite sensual). Make your bedroom, the most alluring place in the house. Occasionally you can even turn the covers back and place an expensive chocolate on your husband's pillow to give him extra energy.

The bed

If you have the money to invest in a gorgeous masterpiece bed, buy it. The investment pays off well.

When choosing the type of bed you would like to have, shop around. Look for bedroom arrangements in furniture stores, catalogs and magazines, and pay attention in the homes of people you visit. For many years I had a dream file filled with pictures of beds I had seen in magazines.

Which style best suits you and your husband? Which is the most attractive? Colonial? Elegant French? Italian? Traditional, Modern, Contemporary? Perhaps you love the wonderful antique beds which create a romantic mood all their own. Is it a style you can live with for many years? This should be a major investment, so make sure it is what you want. But if you have a so-so bed, don't give up on making it look romantic. Add to its beauty whenever you can.

Walls

Bedrooms were called "performance rooms" in the mistress's house a few hundred years ago. I find this term most interesting. Sleeping was done there as well, but the major emphasis in the privacy of that room was on the physical relationship. Detailed murals portraying the love that could be anticipated in the room were found painted above doorways and on the walls.

What do you see displayed on the walls of your bedroom? Something romantic-oriented? Or are they filled with family pictures of your kids beginning at age one through graduation? I personally prefer not to have my children staring at me when I'm being intimate with my husband. If the pictures are there, it is sometimes difficult to free your mind of the motherly feelings that could inhibit you. Reserve the walls of your bedroom for pictures which create the mood for romance.

Our room is very comfortable and inviting. We have chosen art that reflects what we consider romantic. One favorite is Gustav Klimt's painting (a print actually, I wish it were an original!) of "The Kiss". If you know the story of this painting it is very romantic. Klimt is a very sensual artist. I am also one who believes in the beauty of memories. Nostalgia is of utmost importance to me. It helps my heart and mind remember our early days of romance, so I always reserve space in our bedroom for displaying treasures from the past. It is a constant reminder that once upon a time we were head over heels in love and we need to work on safeguarding those feelings now and in the future.

Décor

How you choose to decorate your bedroom will create atmosphere one way or another. Is it presently what you desire it to be? Have you spent more money on rooms in the house that catch visitors' eyes and skimped on decorating your own bedroom?

From the bed, which we have discussed in detail, to the tables you choose, always let the results speak of love. In decorating remember:

- Have a long-range plan.

- Choose your colors and furniture wisely.

- Utilize wallpaper, paint or stenciling.

- Don't forget fresh cut flowers.

- Lighting is important to create mood.

- Try some nostalgia.

- Create a room that is inviting.

- Use candles, mirrors, lamps and treasures from the past.

- Don't allow your bedroom to become a storage room!

- Your bedroom should say in everyway that two people, very much in love, reside here.

Atmosphere

According to Webster, atmosphere is "the mass of air, clouds, gases surrounding the earth and any other place." Through the decades we have come to use the word in a different way. It is the feeling one experiences through sight, sound and smell in the place he inhabits. Much can be said for those who create the right atmosphere before plunging into any important event.

We create some type of atmosphere in and around our home and family every day. We choose what it will be. Does it create a loving mood, or just a blasé nothingness? Creating "the mood" can come through the beauty of art seen in the pictures on the wall. It can be felt through music as the pulsating beat moves through our bodies. Atmosphere can be enhanced by the fragrance of perfumes, scented candles or fresh cut flowers filling the room with an intoxicating desire.

Does your bedroom reveal the sweet, passionate love that two people residing there feel for one another? Or does your room have the atmosphere of an attic storage area or a workroom where all the undone laundry and ironing gets dumped? Take my advice and dump it someplace else. Make your bedroom a true fantasy world for you and your husband!

Personal Challenge for an extraordinary love nest

1. What do you need to do to improve your bed? If you do not have a dream bed pictured, begin your search for one today.

2. Look at the walls of your bedroom. Decide what has to go and what you can use to create a romantic atmosphere. Have at least one bit of nostalgia somewhere. Dig it out and start to enjoy the beauty of memories.

3. How are the colors in this room? Do you need to paint, wallpaper or updated? Remember your file on the perfect bed? Add art that you want to that file as well.

4. Do you need to invest in new sheets, blankets or comforter? Do not allow these to get threadbare before replacing them.

5. Do you have candles, romantic lighting and music available in this room? Work specifically on the

atmosphere you wish to create. Ask yourself, "How does this room make me feel when I walk through the door? Does it say what I want it to about our love for one another? Is it evident that I consider it the most important room in the house? If not, go to work on it today.

The bedroom is just the beginning

One area to keep on the front burner is creativity in romance. Do not settle for the ho-hums in your relationship. Decide today to make yourself undeniably unforgettable, extraordinarily exquisite.

Be Alluring

Yes, I know. You have a hard time seeing yourself quite like that. It's time to change those thoughts. Realize that everyday life can be sexier than you think. Glamour Magazine recently took a survey and found that men find some pretty ordinary situations extremely sensual:

- "A woman pulling on stockings."

- "Watching her put on a necklace or choose earrings."

- "Seeing her fresh from a shower, in a big robe with hair wet and combed back."

- "Watching her have interaction with others (proud that she belongs to me)

I took my own survey and came up with a few more:

- "Watching her walk around in sexy underwear, especially if we are in a hurry and sex is out of the question. I find myself wanting her all day long."

- "Seeing her quietly sitting alone in front of the fire, her thoughts far away."

- "Our skin in water together, like swimming or sharing a spa or shower."

- "Napping on top of the covers, dressed skimpily."

Perhaps it's time to rethink our everyday life. Make the most of the sexy images that happen around us on a regular basis.

My friend Mary says her husband thinks it is very provocative for her to sleep in his T-shirt. Each night she gets out a clean T-shirt he is planning to wear the next day. She puts his favorite perfume on her freshly showered body, then slips into the T-shirt, and wears sexy panties.

Early the next morning she removes the T-shirt, places it with his clean clothes for the day and puts on her robe until she is ready to get dressed. As Mary's husband goes through the day, the delicate scent of her perfume lingers with him and he feels extremely close to her.

Needless to say, Mary is alluring her husband and quite effectively, I might add. I watch them together and can see this man only has eyes for one very smart lady - Mary with that marvelous T-shirt!

Mystery Scent

Something my friend Mary might not even be aware of is *pheromones* - subtle sexual aromas exuded by mammals. In animals, this aroma acts as a mating device. Although humans do not go around smelling people to find a suitable mate, Stephanie Sanders, of the Kinsey Institute for Research in Sex and Gender and Reproduction, says, "Pheromones exert far more influence over us that we realize. A woman's sense of smell sharpens at mid-cycle - which means her ability to detect her partner's pheromones may be heightened during ovulation, when she's both most aroused and less likely to conceive…Sexual scents may underlie the undeniable but unexplainable attraction we feel for certain people we've just met."[ii]

We bathe, use perfumes, powders, deodorants —and still these pheromones seem to affect us. This must be pretty potent stuff. Perhaps Mary's husband is not smelling the bottled perfume, but the sweet small that is uniquely Mary's.

The Song of Solomon speaks of a certain fragrance which the two lovers relish and remember even when apart:

"Pleasing is the fragrance of your perfumes; your name is like perfume poured out" (1:3).

"The fragrance of your perfume is better than any spice" (4:10b).

"The fragrance of your garments is like that of Lebanon" (4:11b).

Many times I have smelled my husband's shirt and felt very stirred up, thinking I would love to have him near me at that moment.

Mary's idea of wearing her husband's T-shirt is one we should all try. I love the idea of my fragrance lingering with my husband Richard all day. Let's make the most of these mysterious pheromones.

Nighties

I can hardly speak of alluring without mentioning the nighties we choose to sleep in each night. Think back to the week of your honeymoon. You probably did some special shopping. We all wanted everything to be perfect those first nights we spent together.

What about now? Why aren't we just a little bit embarrassed when we take out that wretched rag night after night? You know, the one that is so comfy and broken in. Why is it we will spend money for a new coat because the old one is worn out, but continue to wear ragged panties, bras and nightgowns? Do we care more what others think of our appearance than our own husband? Shouldn't he be the one we wish to please?

Marilyn's Story. Marilyn is a friend of mine who shared with me her own sad story of neglect in this area. In the beginning of her marriage, Marilyn had the right idea. She purchased wonderful see-through nightgowns, bras and panties. Great looking stuff for the eyes of her new groom. He loved it! As he thought of her throughout the day, he could remember clearly what she had on underneath her clothing. He enjoyed it continually through the instant replay of his mind. He experienced great pleasure in the reruns he had tucked away. He could relive the sensual beauty of his wife at any time, even when she wasn't around.

When Marilyn was pregnant with her first child, things began to change. She didn't feel that attractive anymore, and she certainly did not enjoy parading around in exotic undergarments in front of her husband. Maternity bras and panties are big, serviceable-looking and comfortable. She wore them throughout her nine months of waiting. After the baby was born, she felt fat and unattractive, not the same alluring person she was before. Besides, she felt very secure - her husband was used to seeing her at her worst, and he stayed around.

About this time Marilyn began to let down in the sensuality department. After all, she was a mother, and the fun and games had to stop for a few years. She planned on returning to it one day…when the children were older.

In the meantime, her husband noticed a real void in his life. He missed seeing his wife dressing and undressing in front of him. The pretty bras and panties were only a fading replay in his mind. He loved Marilyn and wanted to see her in these pretty things once again. The few extra pounds didn't hinder his desire for her. He mentioned this a few times, hoping to convince his wife that he found her as attractive as ever. But by now Marilyn was quite comfortable with the white terrycloth nightgown. Yes, it did have a few snags and stains, but it served the purpose. She was not ready to go back to the see-through material she once donned.

This was unfortunate, because her husband needed *something* to look at. It started out with girlie magazines, nothing too bad. But as always, Satan had a plan. This husband soon found himself interested in pornographic material. All he really wanted was a good look at his loving wife in something besides comfy, worn-out lingerie.

I am not suggesting that we have a gown burning (although some husbands might provide matches if we decided in favor of that). We all have our favorite, warm, snugly jimmies, to be sure. But somewhere we need to have a sexy, see-through, sensual outfit we can pull out. We cannot expect our loving and loyal husband to simply bite the bullet. He has a need to be stimulated by sight. Let's take on the assignment to be his one and only alluring sight.

Be Adventuresome for extraordinary

There lives in all of us a desire for adventure, that playful thing we count on to make life fun and entertaining. We should most definitely integrate adventure into our marriage. Without real thought and planning, it may not come. Adventure rarely happens on a regular basis without someone taking time and effort to help it along.

Couples should look for opportunities in their lives to have some plain ol' fun. Family therapist Michael Metz, of the University of Minnesota Medical School, says, "Playfulness captures the essential features of intimacy. It is vital for healthy interaction."

One study found that the more time couples spent together in activity, such as eating, playing and just talking, the more satisfying the marriage. This same article also mentions that sex is the most powerful source of private play because it allows for experimentation, relaxation and closeness. We must initiate new ways to let go and have fun with each other. That is where adventure comes in. Whether it is frivolous frolic in the park or a well-planned weekend away from home, it is essential to the well-being of our marriages.

I have some true stories to share with you, given to me by women who believe adventure is an important part of their marriage.

Jane's Story: I wanted to do something extra special for my husband on Valentine's Day. Something wild and crazy that he would not soon forget. After much thought and some input from a friend, I struck upon the perfect idea—a balloon dance!

Early on the fourteenth I spent the morning blowing up small balloons of various shapes and sizes. Afterwards, I tied them to several lengths of string and fashioned them into an outfit.

When my husband Tom came home from work we enjoyed a nice meal with our two children and celebrated Valentine's Day as a family. We put the kids to bed early so we could spend the rest of the evening together...alone.

I told Tom to go to the bedroom and he would find a surprise from me under his pillow. Under the pillow I left a set of instructions fastened with a diaper pin. The instructions told him to get ready for bed, hold the diaper pin in his hand, and wait for me to appear.

After a reasonable amount of time, I entered the bedroom humming the song, *The Stripper.* I did a tantalizing dance wearing only my balloon outfit. By that time, the purpose of the diaper pin became quite obvious.

A cute twist to this story is that the diaper pin came in very handy when, in just nine months to the day, we had a delightful baby boy. That was a Valentine's Day my husband would not soon forget!

Janet's Story: My husband Todd's 40th birthday was coming up and I just had to make it unforgettable. He is busy at work, and his schedule is jam packed. He has to plan for weeks in advance for any kind of getaway. So I decided to kidnap him.

I made reservations at a wonderful bed and breakfast place that resembled Tara from *Gone With the Wind.* It was especially fun to go behind his back to rearrange his schedule. Each night I had to check his Day-Timer to make certain his secretary could cancel and appointment on the kidnapping date.

The end of October drew near and the entire staff was in on the kidnapping. We passed notes secretly, make anonymous phone calls and generally had a great time keeping Todd in the dark.

Finally, the big day arrived. I prepared breakfast for the family in usual way, go the kids off to school, and kissed my birthday boy good-bye, wishing him a great day at the office. As soon as he was out of sight, I began to fly through the house, getting his private toiletries packed and ready for our big rendezvous.

I placed the suitcases in the trunk of the car so he would not see them. I dressed up in my very best outfit, and off I went to steal him away.

I arrived around ten o'clock that morning. I knocked on his door, walked in and said I needed him to go somewhere very important with me. He obliged, and out the door we went.

No one in the office let on anything was up. I took the driver's seat; he rode shotgun. I headed straight for the freeway, which unnerved him to some degree. He said, "Hon, what are you doing? Where are we going? You know I have a lot of meetings and appointments today that I need to get back to."I smiled and kept heading straight down the freeway. By this time he was actually sweating. After we had been driving for about an hour (an hour filled with sweet reflections on his 40 years), he figured I was up to no good and had resolved to wait and see where his crazy, impetuous wife of his was taking him. As we pulled up to the mansion, he actually turned white."What is this, Janet? I can't believe my eyes. It looks like something out of a fairy tale," he exclaimed. When the bellhop escorted us to our fabulous bedroom, a throwback to the pre-Civil War days, Todd was elated.

We had an amazing and memorable twenty-four hours. The atmosphere, the adventure and the accommodations were intoxicating. We delighted in each other every possible moment.

He brings up this wonderful day from time to time, and always thanks me for the effort it took to pull off this unforgettable adventure.

I hope these adventures have inspired some of you to come up with a few endeavors of your own for your special man.

A few other ideas:

Leave a steamy note in the shower for him, explaining in detail what you plan on doing to him when he gets home that evening.

When your husband has to go away on a business trip, pack a pair of sexy undies in his suitcase. Hide them among his clothes so he will discover them as he unpacks. (This is especially fun is he is rooming with one of his colleagues.) The undies will keep you on his mind the entire time he is away.

Adventure may take some effort, but the dividends are well worth the time you invest.

Be Allowing

Do you remember the old song "I'm in the Mood for Love?" Well, are you? What gets us in the mood anyway?

Scientists are discovering that there is such a thing as "sexual chemistry." This "chemistry" can, on a daily basis, affect when we feel sexually aroused. It has to do with our hormones. Most women think it is estrogen which governs our desire. But not so, say the experts.

Research psychologist Barbara Sherwin, of McGill University in Montreal, found that the hormone testosterone, known as the male hormone, is responsible for these feelings. You may not have realized it, but women have testosterone in their bodies as well. This hormone is the energizer of our sexual desire. Take it away and the sex drive dies.

Dr. Sherwin will often prescribe testosterone along with estrogen to women who have had a complete hysterectomy. These patients experience a noticeable increase in sexual desire, and report feeling stronger, more energetic and in higher spirits. It appears we do not need an extensive amount of this hormone to make our body function at its best. But we certainly do need it to keep us on an even keel.

Ever wonder why your husband is in the mood in the morning, and you aren't? Because testosterone is at its peak in the morning. We women tend to allow what's going on around us to alter the peak we experience in the morning. We are programmed to get up, get breakfast, get dressed, get the kids dressed, etc. By the time we have done all these things, our peak is already passed.

But all is not in vain. We have a monthly peak as well - twelve to fourteen days after our monthly period begins, which is when we ovulate. Isn't it marvelous how God put us together? He gave us an inborn heightened sexual desire right when we are most likely to conceive. So if you are planning a honeymoon getaway, I would suggest going mid-cycle. Timing can be the deciding factor between a so-so time and a great time away.

Toward the end of your menstrual cycle a neurotransmitter called serotonin kicks in and acts like a sexual suppressant. So there really are times you just don't feel like having sex.

I can hear some of the yeas and hoorahs right about now: "I finally have an excuse to say no and not feel bad about it." Not exactly. Our sexual relationship is a gift we can give to each other. As 1 Corinthians 7 tells us, our body belongs to our husband and his body belongs to us. Sex between husband and wife is to be given as a gift - not demanded, withheld or used as a reward or punishment.

My husband has a friend who walks on egg shells constantly. His wife tells him he had better comply with all her wishes or there will be no sex. He is one frustrated individual.

Using sex as a means of getting things your way is a very selfish act. Sometimes you may not be super turned-on to the idea of a romp in the hay, but this is the time to put aside your feelings. Put your effort into satisfying his needs. Allow your husband to enjoy you and your marvelous love - love that you alone are allowed by our Father to give your husband. You may be surprised how this can put you in the mood.

Being married doesn't mean the fun has to stop. Take a chance. Buy a skimpy little nightie and surprise your husband tonight. Plan a getaway for the two of you and then do it. Rekindle the romance of your love. You'll be on your way to a happier, long-lasting extraordinary relationship.

May I suggest?

1. Try to incorporate at least one of the everyday sensual images listed at the beginning of this chapter into your daily routine.

2. Look closely at your lingerie. If you do not have something very sexy and alluring, go shopping!

3. If you do not have something sexy in your lingerie drawer, great. Why not get a little crazy? Buy that outrageous looking red teddy or black bikini underpanties. Spice up your same ol' tune.

4. Plan in detail an exciting adventure for you and your husband, then carry it out. Don't ever, ever top planning adventure for your relationship.

5. Monitor your mood swings and determine when you think your testosterone is at its peak. Use this information in planning dates with your husband. If you have had a hysterectomy and feel out of sorts most of the time, check with your gynecologist regarding possible hormone treatment.

Marriages today are at risk, since more than half will not make it to a 50 year anniversary. That being said, we must do everything in our power to keep love and romance at the top of our priority list. Marriage is a lot more than sexual love, but it is not complete without it. It is God's plan to meet the God given sexual appetite that lives within each of us satisfied. (Now yours or your husband may need that appetite revived up, if so, work on it…it does matter.)

Just For Him

Men should certainly read and take into consideration everything suggested up to this point, but I have also put together a few things just for them to do:

1. Be thoughtful! When buying a gift for your wife, don't just purchase something at the last minute. Make mental notes throughout everyday conversations when she mentions something she would like to have …someday. Then, we you have the money, get it for her. This will say in deeds, not just words that you actually listen to her, which brings up the next point.

2. Listen. Most of the time when your wife cries on your shoulder, she does not want you to fix anything. She simply wants you to listen intently and validate her distress, even if you think it is a small thing, listen and agree with her pain! That's all, nothing more.

111

3. Make plans for date night on your own. This will show some forethought and that you were actually thinking about it before the two of you got into the car to leave. You can make this a simple jester and tell her earlier in the day where you will be going and when. Or, you can tantalize her with keeping it a secret dropping hints all week. Do this once in a while and you will earn a lot of points in the romantic department.

4. Do deeds of kindness without her asking. If you know something around the house needs to be done, do it. This would certainly cut down on the "nagging" so many men complain of. This also frees time up for her to be rested and ready when you want her full of interest and energy when it comes to lovemaking.

5. Tell her you love her, say it often. Women's number one need is to feel secure, and you aid her in feeling secure by assuring her of your love in actions and in words. Do not assume she knows you love her, tell her!

We must work to achieve extraordinary in our lives. Relationships are no exception. You cannot have a marriage that is extraordinary without putting genuine effort into it that is above and beyond what the average person is willing to invest.

Chapter 8

Extraordinary Differences

Opposites attract! That's what they say, and it is generally true. A fun-loving party animal will usually marry a well-organized bore. A controlling workaholic will end up with a peaceful, non-aggressive person. Why?

Perhaps we see something in the other person that we lack within ourselves. The playful, free spirit knows he needs someone to get him in shape and keep him on track. Finding this person will give him more time to talk, hop and skip through life while the well-organized one keeps it all together for him. The controlling workaholic doesn't want to be bothered with keeping peace, so the calm and collected spouse is needed to make up for his insensitivity.

We generally do not think about this when we are dating our spouse-to-be. But soon after the wedding bells cease to ring, we realize we are joined with someone completely different from ourselves. Then the fun begins!

Author and speaker Florence Littauer has

greatly expanded on the four basic personality types discovered by Hippocrates: sanguine, choleric, melancholy, and phlegmatic. These words are new to many of us, so we are going to take a closer look at just how the different personality types affect our marriage relationship.

Florence Littauer, in her book Personality Plus, has renamed the four personalities according to the particular trait which is most descriptive. Sanguines have a need to be *popular;* cholerics are *powerful;* melancholies must have things *perfect;* the phlegmatics prefers to have *peace.*

Most of us have one predominate personality type with a second one that influences us as well. On the next few pages I've included Fred and Florence Littauer's "Personality Profile" to help you discover what personality combination you are. Take the time right now to go through this profile, making a list of your strengths and weaknesses. After you've finished, you might ask your spouse to take it. Just remember different does not mean wrong.

PERSONALITY PROFILE

DIRECTIONS – In <u>each</u> of the following rows of <u>four words across,</u> place an **X** in front of the <u>one</u> word that most often applies to you. Continue through all forty lines. Be sure each number is marked. If you are not sure of which word "most applies," ask a spouse or a friend.

STRENGTHS

1. ___Adventurous	___Adaptable	___Animated	___Analytical
2. ___Persistent	___Playful	___Persuasive	___Peaceful
3. ___Submissive	___Self-sacrificing	___Sociable	___Strong-willed
4. ___Considerate	___Controlled	___Competitive	___Convincing
5. ___Refreshing	___Respectful	___Reserved	___Resourceful
6. ___Satisfied	___Sensitive	___Self-reliant	___Spirited
7. ___Planner	___Patient	___Positive	___Promoter
8. ___Sure	___Spontaneous	___Scheduled	___Shy
9. ___Orderly	___Obliging	___Outspoken	___Optimistic
10. ___Friendly	___Faithful	___Funny	___Forceful
11. ___Daring	___Delightful	___Diplomatic	___Detailed
12. ___Cheerful	___Consistent	___Cultured	___Confident
13. ___Idealistic	___Independent	___Inoffensive	___Inspiring
14. ___Demonstrative	___Decisive	___Dry humor	___Deep
15. ___Mediator	___Musical	___Mover	___Mixes easily
16. ___Thoughtful	___Tenacious	___Talker	___Tolerant
17. ___Listener	___Loyal	___Leader	___Lively
18. ___Contented	___Chief	___Chartmaker	___Cute
19. ___Perfectionist	___Pleasant	___Productive	___Popular
20. ___Bouncy	___Bold	___Behaved	___Balanced

115

WEAKNESSES

21. ___Blank ___Bashful ___Brassy ___Bossy

22. ___Undisciplined ___Unsympathetic ___Unenthusiastic ___Unforgiving

23. ___Reticent ___Resentful ___Resistant ___Repetitious

24. ___Fussy ___Fearful ___Forgetful ___Frank

25. ___Impatient ___Insecure ___Indecisive ___Interrupts

---

26. ___Unpopular ___Uninvolved ___Unpredictable ___Unaffectionate

27. ___Headstrong ___Haphazard ___Hard to please ___Hesitant

28. ___Plain ___Pessimistic ___Proud ___Permissive

29. ___Angered easily ___Aimless ___Argumentative ___Alienated

30. ___Naïve ___Negative attitude ___Nervy ___Nonchalant

---

31. ___Worrier ___Withdrawn ___Workaholic ___Wants credit

32. ___Too sensitive ___Tactless ___Timid ___Talkative

33. ___Doubtful ___Disorganized ___Domineering ___Depressed

34. ___Inconsistent ___Introvert ___Intolerant ___Indifferent

35. ___Messy ___Moody ___Mumbles ___Manipulative

---

36. ___Slow ___Stubborn ___Show-off ___Skeptical

37. ___Loner ___Lord over ___Lazy ___Loud

38. ___Sluggish ___Suspicious ___Short-tempered ___Scatterbrained

39. ___Revengeful ___Restless ___Reluctant ___Rash

40. ___Compromising ___Critical ___Crafty ___Changeable

NOW TRANSFER ALL YOUR X's TO THE CORRESPONDING WORDS ON THE PERSONALITY SCORING SHEET AND ADD UP YOUR TOTALS.

STRENGTHS

SANGUINE POPULAR	CHOLERIC POWERFUL	MELANCHOLY PERFECT	PHLEGMATIC PEACEFUL
1. ___Animated	___Adventurous	___Analytical	___Adaptable
2. ___Playful	___Persuasive	___Persistent	___Peaceful
3. ___Sociable	___Strong-willed	___Self-sacrificing	___Submissive
4. ___Convincing	___Competitive	___Considerate	___Controlled
5. ___Refreshing	___Resourceful	___Respectful	___Reserved
6. ___Spirited	___Self-reliant	___Sensitive	___Satisfied
7. ___Promoter	___Positive	___Planner	___Patient
8. ___Spontaneous	___Sure	___Scheduled	___Shy
9. ___Optimistic	___Outspoken	___Orderly	___Obliging
10. ___Funny	___Forceful	___Faithful	___Friendly
11. ___Delightful	___Daring	___Detailed	___Diplomatic
12. ___Cheerful	___Confident	___Cultured	___Consistent
13. ___Inspiring	___Independent	___Idealistic	___Inoffensive
14. ___Demonstrative	___Decisive	___Deep	___Dry humor
15. ___Mixes easily	___Mover	___Musical	___Mediator
16. ___Talker	___Tenacious	___Thoughtful	___Tolerant
17. ___Lively	___Leader	___Loyal	___Listener
18. ___Cute	___Chief	___Chart maker	___Contented
19. ___Popular	___Productive	___Perfectionist	___Pleasant
20. ___Bouncy	___Bold	___Behaved	___Balanced

TOTALS ___   ___   ___   ___

117

WEAKNESSES

SANGUINE POPULAR	CHOLERIC POWERFUL	MELANCHOLY PERFECT	PHLEGMATIC PEACEFUL
21. ___Brassy	___Bossy	___Bashful	___Blank
22. ___Undisciplined	___Unsympathetic	___Unforgiving	___Unenthusiastic
23. ___Repetitious	___Resistant	___Resentful	___Reticent
24. ___Forgetful	___Frank	___Fussy	___Fearful
25. ___Interrupts	___Impatient	___Insecure	___Indecisive
26. ___Unpredictable	___Unaffectionate	___Unpopular	___Uninvolved
27. ___Haphazard	___Headstrong	___Hard to please	___Hesitant
28. ___Permissive	___Proud	___Pessimistic	___Plain
29. ___Angered easily	___Argumentative	___Alienated	___Aimless
30. ___Naïve	___Nervy	___Negative attitude	___Nonchalant
31. ___Wants credit	___Workaholic	___Withdrawn	___Worrier
32. ___Talkative	___Tactless	___Too sensitive	___Timid
33. ___Disorganized	___Domineering	___Depressed	___Doubtful
34. ___Inconsistent	___Intolerant	___Introvert	___Indifferent
35. ___Messy	___Manipulative	___Moody	___Mumbles
36. ___Show-off	___Stubborn	___Skeptical	___Slow
37. ___Loud	___Lord-over-others	___Loner	___Lazy
38. ___Scatterbrained	___Short tempered	___Suspicious	___Sluggish
39. ___Restless	___Rash	___Revengeful	___Reluctant
40. ___Changeable	___Crafty	___Critical	___Compromising

TOTALS ____   ____   ____   ____

COMBINED
TOTALS ____   ____   ____   ____

*The Personality Profile is reprinted with permission from its author, Fred Littauer.

Different is Not Wrong

Two very different people will not flow together without turbulence from time to time. Knowing which personality you are and identifying that of your husband will help you understand and accept the differences in each other. Most importantly, *different* doesn't mean *wrong*. Sometimes we make the foolish mistake of trying to change the other person into who we are, to make them more acceptable to us. This will only lead to frustration.

Joe met Sandy, a bouncy cheerleader, who was full of life, fun and frivolous talk. She accepted every invitation to any gathering where people would be. He watched her weave her winsome way into each and every heart in the room. He loved her energy. This attracted him since his own introverted personality kept him from going to all of the fun things at school. With Sandy around, he didn't even have to talk. She did enough for both of them.

They had a fabulous wedding, and then fled to the quaint cottage Joe had chosen for the honeymoon. Right away Joe began trying to quiet Sandy down. Now that they were adults, certain things would have to shape up in Sandy's life. No more fun. Life had to get serious. Says who? Says Joe!

He spent the next five years organizing, shushing, and lecturing Sandy on how to grow up and lead a peaceful, perfect existence as an adult. Only one problem! Sandy was not a quiet, calm introvert like Joe. Soon the battles began. Sandy continued to go off to parties - alone now, because Joe hated crowds. He despised the way she ignored schedules or kept messy and untidy drawers at home. She seemed so undisciplined.

On the other hand, Joe was boring Sandy to death. He absolutely refused to go to exciting and different places. He was a tightwad, tense and terribly critical. This was not fun anymore.

Joe gave Sandy an ultimatum: "Change your way or I'm out of here." Sandy gave in to save her marriage. She lived her life Joe's way for fifteen years.

But Sandy was always miserable. She spent each day living a life that wasn't her own. This sent her into a deep depression. One blue Monday morning Sandy took a handful of pills hoping to end her misery.

I lived only a few blocks from Sandy at the time and as I passed by her house her son came running out screaming. Jamie had come home from school to find his mother unconscious. She was barely breathing.

The paramedics arrived in time to revive this lady who at one time in her life had been so vivacious.

Joe had literally drained from Sandy her desire for living. He insisted on changing her from the beautiful creation God intended to the creation Joe demanded.

Romans 15:7 says, *"Accept one another, just as Christ accepted you."* Are you trying to change someone? Make them into another you? Does your marriage really need two of you? The verse in Romans says to accept - not rearrange, not fix up, not overhaul, not redesign! *Being different doesn't mean being wrong.*

Blending It Instead of Blowing It

Are you married to a **popular** who is driving you nuts because he loves to be with people? Are you a **powerful** constantly pushing a **peaceful** beyond his limits?

The only person you can change is yourself. Accept and appreciate your spouse for who he is and be willing to make some changes in your life to help him cope with you. Look long and hard at your weaknesses and see how they might irritate and annoy your husband. Here are a few typical examples of problem areas in the personality types.

If you are a **popular**, you'll need to control the chatter once in a while. Give the house some peace and quiet. Learn to put your husband's clothes away in a neat and orderly way. Plan a quiet vacation on occasion and try to enjoy it. Keep the facts as accurate as possible and try to control spending.

Popular Patty always had to be on the phone, on her way out the door or have guests over for dinner. This leaves little time to clean, wash clothes or cook meals. Her household is always in an uproar. This makes her timid, fearing, **peaceful** daughter insecure. It drives her meticulous **perfect** husband right up the wall. Patty needs to make some changes for the sake of the other members in her family. She doesn't need to become a different person, just more sensitive and less selfish.

If you are the **powerful** one, try not to be so bossy, impatient or quick-tempered. You need to let your spouse have his way once in a while. Learn to give compliments in a gracious way. Practice saying, "I'm sorry…I was wrong." Realize you don't have to control every situation.

Bob is Mr. Powerful. He runs a giant corporation with many people obeying his every command. When at home he continues to snap out orders. This controlling spirit carries over into many areas of his life. Bob has to control all social activities. He decides *when* everyone will get together, *where* they will get together and *what* the conversation will be while there! This causes people to refuse his invitations (when they have a choice, that is).

If you are the **perfect** personality, you put others at a disadvantage. Whatever the tasks, or whoever you're with, you will always find imperfections. Stop being so critical and negative as this gets you nowhere. Don't become moody if you haven't checked everything off your list for the day or is some *person* (you could do without most people, anyway) messes up your schedule. Allow for imperfection, especially in yourself.

Pricilla Perfect is well meaning, but she drives her husband crazy, scurrying right behind him, tidying up or redoing the tasks he has already done. She warns him constantly of the horrible things that can go wrong in his latest venture as she continues checking off her list of "Things To Do Today." She will sulk for days over something her spouse said and she seems determined to stay in the pit of depression once she's there.

If the personality profile revealed that you are a

peaceful, you may need to be a little more enthusiastic about life in general. Others may constantly try to get you motivated. You have a lot of fears and one is the fear of *change*. You get in a rut easily, so make an effort to give your spouse a little spice once in a while.

Quite often Peggy Peaceful asks me to go shopping with her to help her decide on a new dress. She can't seem to make up her mind on her own. She told me the other day that she wanted to change her furniture around in the living room, but could not decide just how she wanted it. I asked her how long the furniture had been arranged like it is now. She said, "Oh, I don't know., probably around twelve years or so." Peggy needs to dare to be different and do it without delay.

Emotional Needs - Enough to Go Around

We all have very different emotional needs. We probably had no idea how to meet the needs of our spouses, so we usually end up giving *them* what *we* need emotionally, thinking they are quite happy with that.

Cheri is a **popular** and her husband Tony is a **perfect/powerful**, When they got married at ages eighteen and twenty, they had no idea they were so different. They struggled to meet each other's emotional needs.

One of the ways they failed was on birthdays. Every year Cheri, the **popular**, would plan the biggest blowout of the decade for Tony, her **perfect/powerful** husband.

She would have balloons in every shape and size, loud music, tons of food and of course, lots and lots of people. What person in his right mind would not love a rollicking birthday like the one Cheri could put together?

That's right, a **perfect**. So Tony, in great pain, would smile faintly through the ordeal as Cheri laughed gaily and entertained the guests. (Someone had to, since the guest of honor was being most ungrateful for all the work done just for him.) Cheri would end up crying because he didn't have a good time, and he would be hurt that she could not understand his needs.

Cheri's birthday was in June. She would grow more excited as each day passed in June, knowing that soon it would be her birthday. This was the day she was to be spoiled, surprised and surrounded by all the hundreds of people who loved her.

Cheri was surprised all right. There was never any big surprise and certainly no people. Just a quiet dinner for two in a nice restaurant with a practical gift that came with a guarantee.

Why couldn't Tony give Cheri the birthday that she wanted, just once? Why? Because he was giving her the kind of birthday *he* wanted every year. It took them a while to catch on, but in time they got pretty good at planning the perfect birthday for each other.

So You're Not the Perfect Match?

Communication patterns for varied combinations of **popular**, **powerful**, **peaceful** and **perfect** will vary. Below I've given some tips to help you and your mate work together despite your differences. Find your personality trait, and then look for your mate's.

If you are the **powerful** and your husband is
* **Popular**, you need to:
Reduce emphasis on results. Learn to compliment and praise him publicly, Increase your ability to laugh and have a good time.

- **Peaceful**, you need to:
Take time to listen to him. You must give him the opportunity to prove his self-worth, *his* way. Refrain from pushing too hard. Give him the place of authority in your home.

- **Powerful**, you need to:
Allow your husband his area of authority and stay out of his territory. If he doesn't ask for advice, keep it to yourself. Don't play tug of war for power. Learn to give him a lot of appreciation for his accomplishments.

- **Perfect**, you need to:
Slow down and pay more attention to details. He wants to be thorough in situations. Allow him this right. Learn to be more sensitive to his emotions. Give him space to be left alone from time to time.

If you are the **popular** and your husband is
- **Powerful**, you need to:
Work harder for results. Be sure to follow through. Be sincere when giving praise. He needs to know you really *are* impressed with his work.

- **Popular**, you need to:
Stop grandstanding and calling so much attention to yourself. Allow him to be the life of the party

too. Make big efforts to compliment and praise him publicly in every area of life.

• **Peaceful**, you need to:
Stop dragging him to every party in town. Understand that he will never show emotions as much as you, so stop being disappointed. Think of ways to encourage his dry sense of humor. Rest in the quiet he can bring to your life.

• **Perfect**, you need to:
Be more exact and think about what you are saying. Be tidier, thrifty and respect his lists of "to do's." Do not joke when he is hurting. A joke will only make the hurt worse.

If you are **peaceful** and your husband is
• **Powerful**, you need to:
Stop rambling and say what you mean. Stand up for yourself. He needs for you to be strong or he will walk all over you. Make a decision and stick with it.

• **Popular**, you need to:
Add some spice to your life. You will grow very boring if you do not make this effort. Go with him to most of his fun things. Don't be content to send him out alone. Speed up some.

- **Perfect**, you need to:
Make rational choices *on your own*. Be the aggressive one on occasion. If you aren't watchful, this marriage will become very dull and clinical.

- **Peaceful**, you need to:
Get motivated and help your husband realize his potential as well. He needs to feel he's worth something - help him see that he is. Make a big effort to talk and share with him.

If you are **perfect** and your husband is
- **Powerful**, you need to:
Cut all the details and give him straight answers. Allow him the right to do his job his way, even if it isn't perfect. Learn to give him appreciation without a negative footnote added.

- **Popular**, you need to:
Learn to relax and laugh when he's telling a not-so-factual story. He needs to hear a lot of praise from you in his success. Do not critique him to death.

- **Peaceful**, you need to:
Strive for openness. Allow him time to make decisions. Watch that you don't organize the life out of your marriage. Respect his true fears.

- **Perfect**, you need to:

Watch that your marriage doesn't become a contest of trying to out-chart and out-list each other. Try being spontaneous from time to time. Do not let your marriage become too predictable. Enjoy those long, meaningful talks you can have together.

Sexuality by Personality

Each of the four personality types respond in their own way to intimacy. Each will vary due to past influences. If home life was not good for you or your spouse or perhaps the model you had to observe was warped, or if there was abuse of some type, your personality's natural sexual response could be suppressed. If you or your spouse are experiencing serious sexual problems, you need to talk it through and perhaps seek professional help.

A **popular** usually wants lovemaking to be fun! He will want variety, so make sure you give it to him. The **popular** can have a real problem with being faithful, because he loves attention from someone new. Give him a lot of attention and variety. Spontaneity is supreme. Forget the formula and get on with the fun and the grand finale.

The **perfect**, on the other hand, will tend to "do it by the book." He loves music and atmosphere. Making love is very serious business to the **perfect**. So is commitment. He would think it through very carefully before he would ever stray.

A **powerful** will want to be in control, deciding when, where and how you will make love. He is more interested in the results than how he goes about it. He may even seem regimental at times. **Powerfuls** are generally people of great passions.

The **peaceful** wants very much to please his lover, but will have a difficult time deciding just how that might be done and then doing it. He will most certainly need someone to be aggressive and get things going, but once begun he aims to please. He would never hurry through this special time, and would give you all the time needed.

Working on it works!

I have friends who have been married sixteen years. Recently, things had been going very poorly in their marriage. He was constantly upset and disappointed in her, and she was miserable for letting him down. They were totally unaware of what the other needed emotionally. I recommended that they read together Florence Littauer's two books, *Personality Plus* and *Your Personality Tree*. They spent an entire weekend absorbed in these books.

I received a call the next week from the woman and she was singing a brand new song of love. She said, "Pamala, reading those books opened up a new world to us. We are closer than we ever thought possible, and a new love is taking shape in our hearts. Thank you! Thank Florence for us! We will never be the same because of what she revealed in her books on personalities."

I highly recommend these two books. Much of my research on this subject has come from Florence's wisdom which I gleaned from her lectures as well as *Personality Plus* and *Your Personality Tree*. You can find these in your local Christian bookstore.

Some suggestions for accepting differences

1. First determine what your main temperament is. Then have your husband do the same.

2. Write down on a piece of paper the weaknesses you are aware of in yourself.

3. Now go back to each weakness and decide what

you can do to keep this weakness from becoming a source of irritation in your relationship.

4. This is a great time to find out from your husband if you have been meeting his emotional needs, or are you been giving to him what **you** have been needing yourself? The most beautiful discovery in all of this information is that *different* doesn't mean *wrong*. Look at your husband's differences and repeat several times, *Different doesn't mean he is wrong.*

Chapter 9

Loving Extraordinary

God made our hearts to love; without love from family and friends life will be long and lonely here on earth. One verse in the Bible that separates the authentic Christian from the person just going through the motions is, John13:35. *"Everyone will know you are my disciples if you love one another."* If loving each other is defining of a Jesus follower, why aren't we better at it? Why don't we love one another more? It certainly is more appealing than the reputation of always arguing about one thing and another. How many times have you heard a non believer applaud the way Christians love each other?

If seems we are quick to judge our brothers and sisters who also call themselves Christians, and do not see things exactly like we do. What if God only measured out grace to us in proportion to the grace we give others? How much grace would you deserve? I decided a long time ago that I would need a lot of grace from God in this life, so I began giving it out in abundance. I call it giving people a lot of spandex. We are all human, not divine, we will make huge mistakes occasionally; we need grace and we need to give grace. There are ugly things inside of us that only God knows about. The worst things about us are not those things that people can see, but it is the secrets in our soul, the unseen, that unknown wrongdoing that you would not dare to mention to anyone, that God sees and forgives. Remember that grace given to you when extending grace to others in love.

God gives us the gift of friends to help get us through life. Recently my husband Troy and I heard a great teaching from Pastor Rob Thompson's "Ten Laws of Relationship". After listening to his teaching on this subject, we decided we should develop our own list of laws before we allowed anyone into our inner circle of close friends. I have a few of ours listed, however I encourage you to think and pray about what you want in your closest of friends, and then be true to those desires.

1. They must believe and uphold the same morals and values that we do.

2. They must be loyal and trustworthy with confidences.

3. They must not gossip or be jealous

4. They must be truth tellers in love and receive the same from us.

5. They must encourage us to be our best and celebrate our successes.

6. We want to make time for these friends, however time is not a measurement we use for the level of commitment of love we have for each other. Time will never separate us.

Loving when you get nothing in return

My son Aaron gave me a great lesson about loving and giving to others when there would be absolutely no reward except the doing of it. When Aaron was fifteen he went with his youth group to work in Chicago with homeless people who lived in the inner city. Parents were informed that this would be a very hard mission for these teens, but life changing. I had to sign a release agreement for Aaron to participate. When they arrived at their destination, (previously unknown to them, by the way), they got off the bus with the clothes they had on their backs and $5 in their pockets. They were told they must survive for the weekend making due with what they had or what they could find. They had to live with the homeless people and if they got the chance, minister to them. I do not know what took place that weekend in Aaron's life, but it was indeed life changing!

When I arrived at the church to pick him up, he no longer had the coat he left with, nor his very nice long sleeved shirt, nor his warm socks and expensive shoes. He walked toward me wearing a skimpy white tee shirt and jeans, and the brightest smile I've ever seen. Also he had something new that he has had ever since that day…the biggest heart I have ever known anyone to possess. He gives and loves with very little expectation in return. His friends have told me time and time again of the food he has given to strangers, often times buying a meal for a young man or woman digging through garbage barrels at restaurants. He is known for offering shelter to people with no place to stay. He shops at Salvation Army when he can and could care less about designer brands. He is loved by all and when I meet people who know my son, they always leave saying the same thing…Aaron has the biggest heart of anyone I've ever met!

Loving during difficult times

Perhaps you would like to be the kind of friend who encourages and is truly supportive of a family going through a difficult time, a divorce or logterm illness; but you are unsure of what to do or how you should go about it. I have put together a helpful "to do" and "not to do" list for those who truly want to help. Please take time to look over the suggestions below, choose a few that you can implement in the life of a person or family in need. Someone desperately needs your love in action today.

1.   When asking, "How are you?" refuse to accept a "fine" answer. Always follow up with another question. Probe, without prying, for the truth.

2.   Work to keep in touch throughout the longevity of the crisis. Don't quit. Too often the "out of sight, out of mind" rule applies. It takes work to be a true friend. *"There are 'friends' who destroy each other, but a real friend sticks closer than a brother."* (Proverbs 18:24 NLT) Job himself said, *"A despairing man should have the devotion of his friends"* (6:14)

3.   Send an e-mail or card (humorous as well as inspirational).

4.   Telephone them; a short conversation is all that is needed.

5.   Be the aggressor in the friendship. Just dealing

with the stress of an illness or loss takes so much energy that little is left to seek out the much needed friendships at this time. Proverbs 17:17 states, *"A friend loves at all times, and a brother is born for adversity."*

6.   Be thoughtful. Offer to pick up some groceries, a pizza, scrub a shower, rake the leaves, etc. Look for practical ways to help and then do them. Most people in need are not very comfortable asking for help.

7.   Include their family in as many social activities as you can. Exclusion and isolation are common problems for the healthy members of the family.

8.   Remember to check on the caregiver. Ask how they are doing and offer to take them out on occasion.

9.   Be on their side. Do not criticize them or the decisions they must make. Unless you have personally been in their exact situation, you really don't know what you would do.

10.   Listen more than you talk. Sometimes all that is needed is companionship. Take something you can do with your friend. Perhaps you can just sit and read to them, rent a movie, or listen to their favorite music.

11. Offer hope with love and compassion, not judgment or criticism.

12. Say something about the fact that they are suffering. Ignoring the obvious is awkward. Say, "I wish I knew the right thing to say, but I care and I am here if you need me."

13. Pray for them and their family. Pray for courage, energy, rest, peace, and for specific needs like financial resources, wisdom, understanding, coping with pain, etc. *"Carry each other's burdens, and in this way you will fulfill the law of Christ." (Galatians 6:2)*

14. Try to exude joy in their presence; smiles are contagious!

15. Avoid telling them what you would do if you were in their shoes.

16. Don't feel compelled to share every "cure" you've heard of for their illness. It's insulting and implies that they haven't been doing their own "homework."

17. Be aware of the fact that illness is not just a matter of attitude. Beware of telling people that they just need to have more faith.

18. Respect their limitations. Unless you are the

person's therapist, don't try and push them beyond their comfort level.

19. Remember special occasions, like birthdays. You can always brightens somebody's day by simply remembering little things.

20. **DWYSYWD**. That's short for "do what you said you would do." If you tell the person you will call them tomorrow—call them tomorrow. They are counting on you to keep your word.

Loving others in deeds not just words really proves authentic love. Love! Regardless if it is returned or not. This kind of love is extraordinary and will be remembered about you long after you are gone. Gone from a place you worked, gone from the place you use to live, and eventually gone from this earth. How do you want your loving to be remembered?

Chapter 10

God Is Even Above Extraordinary

God Is God

When considering God and who He is there are many ideas; this chapter is not meant to prove God exists, but rather a substantiation of how huge, vast, and absolutely indescribable the God I believe in is. "God is great; God is good, let us thank Him for this food." Sound familiar? The type of food was only incidental, what matters in this simple prayer is admitting to the nature and character of God Himself. In saying this prayer we acknowledge the fact that every good gift always originates with Him and He exudes greatness. These two truths are irreducible. You cannot have one without the other. A God who is great but not good would be a tyrant, dictator, or despot. A God who is good, but not great, would be a cosmic teddy bear, someone to hold your hand, but powerless to do anything about your circumstances.

God Is Good

These two things are constantly being called into question. *Is* God great? *Is* God good? The headlines cry out and the talking heads in the media feel as though it is their right - their *responsibility* - to put God on the witness stand. In times of tragedy, people wonder why a *good* God would allow a tsunami to wipe out thousands of lives and displace millions of people. God is daily asked to raise His right hand and swear to tell the truth, the whole truth, and nothing but the truth, so help Him…Himself. Oh, they don't come right out and say it, but their questions imply that somehow God is either not good or not great. Goodness is excellence of quality. God not only *does* good deeds, He *is* good. The psalmist said, *"The Lord is good to all; he has compassion on all he has made"* (145:9). This implies to me that He does spare us much more than not. God is so far above us that we cannot begin to understand all of His ways.

As a parent there were times, from my children's perspective, they thought I was being mean. Being children they did not have my experience, knowledge and wisdom. If they did they would know that I was actually sparing them a lot of pain and heartache. I was protecting them from something they could not see or understand. There certainly were times I allowed them a little pain to learn a long-lasting lesson. Once leaned, when something more dangerous came along, they were spared more painful, perhaps even deadly consequences. At the time, they did not think I was demonstrating love to them. They kicked, screamed and cried, feeling I was being hard on them intentionally. But my actions revealed the opposite – my love! This is only an example and even a weak one, given the fact that I am human and have limits. God has none!

God is Great

The word "great" is greatly overused: our coffee is great, our job is great and our kids are great. Theologians have come up with the word "omnipotent" to describe the greatness of God. It means all-powerful. The power or greatness of God is seen in these distinct characteristics:

1. Creativity: by God's power He created all things. The Psalmist proclaimed, *"For when he spoke, the world began. It appeared at his command"* (33:9). As we look into the sky we too must admit that Psalm 19:1-4 is telling the truth! *"The heavens are telling the glory of God, they are a marvelous display of His craftsmanship...without a sound or word, silent in the skies, their message reaches out to the world."*

I must speak of these marvelous displays in

the heavens. Recently I heard a message by Louie Giglio titled, "How Great Is Our God." I have taken the liberty to share with you from his message that presents a scientific view on the greatness of our universe. Thirty-one million light years from earth (FYI: light travels at 186,000 miles per second, to put this distance in perspective) there is a galaxy called, Whirlpool Galaxy. It contains over 300 billion stars, and Whirlpool Galaxy is only one of 100's of billions of galaxies in the universe. Our sun is a star and it is 93 million miles away from us, yet it takes just seconds for its rays to arrive to earth. The sun is 10,000 degrees Fahrenheit on the surface and it is 1 million times larger than the earth. But the sun is a small star compared to millions of others in our universe.

I will give one other example and leave the rest for you to look up on your own, because our universe is such a miraculous phenomenon; it would take more than a paragraph to truly describe it. This small description cannot do it justice. The largest star that scientists have discovered at this writing is called, Canas Majorus. Our earth could fit inside this star 7 quadrillion times! If the earth were the size of a golf ball, this star would be the size of Mt Everest, which is the highest point on the earth! Now re-read the verse about how God spoke all of this into being. God's greatness is indescribable! (For your information: Louie Giglio www.268generation.com)

2. Authority: God's greatness is also seen in His complete authority. Gravity is an undeniable law of God. I do not like it, but if I deny it, I will get hurt. People can rebel against God's authority, but in the end, perhaps theirs, all will see He is the final authority. When you learn to trust His love, respecting His authority comes much easier. He loves us and expresses this love to us in many ways.

One way He has expressed love to each of us is complete forgiveness of sin. Sin is breaking the laws of God our Creator. These laws, as revealed in Scripture, are not meant to impose misery on us, rather to protect us. This forgiveness comes to us through His sinless Son Jesus. God so loved His creation that He sacrificed His most precious Son upon a cross, crucified at the hands of men, men that He was dying for. His death paid in full, a debt of sin that all of mankind has contributed to for all time – past, present, and future (Rom. 5:12; 2 Cor. 5:21). All we have to do is ask for this sacrifice to include us. We receive our forgiveness by faith in the fact that God's Son died for us, and confess that we are sorry for all our sins (John 3:16-18). When you and I have accepted this perfect provision, we can rest in the peace and assurance that we are unconditionally loved by God and that He no longer holds our sins against us, but looks to the sacrifice of his Son's life as payment in full. Although we may stumble along the way from time to time and we will, He will never leave us.

God Is Trustworthy

The more someone or something proves to be trustworthy, the more trust is possible. But what is trust anyway? Recently I was asked to define *trust*. As I pondered the word I concluded it was not easy to define and even harder to put into practice. Webster defines the word trust as, "Assured reliance on the character, ability, strength, or truth of someone or something; having confidence placed in one; or something committed into the care of another."

As I attempted to define trust I developed an acrostic that I want to share with you. This acrostic has been developed over a period of time through my own experiences of learning to trust God and His word. Learning to trust is a process. This is a key point. The more someone or something proves to be trustworthy, the more trust is possible.

T stands for: Taking hold of God's hand, and letting go of what is in mine. There is no way to take hold of something with a full grip with something else in your hand. To attain the best grip, the hand must be free of other things. Most of us do not like to let go of something that is in full view and in our control for something that may or may not be within reach. Trust cannot be accomplished without using a measure of faith. Faith is not fully seeing, yet believing just the same. Let me say again, the more someone proves trustworthy, the more you will trust. God is absolutely trustworthy, even if you cannot see what He is doing at the time. In the end, it is right on.

Are you holding on to something, or someone who needs to be let go of, to gain something far greater for them or yourself? There will be freedom in this purposeful action. Just as a stranded man on the side of a mountain barely holding on to a small tree stump must let go of the stump to grab a rescuer's rope, so must we at times take that same chance to gain true freedom in life.

The next letter in the acrostic for trust is R. R stands for the word resting; resting in, instead of wrestling with. There comes a moment of truth when we are called to trust in the decision we must make; to be at peace with what needs to be done…and then rest in that decision.

When my former husband was diagnosed with a terminal brain disease, I was faced with one dreadful decision after another. I did not choose this assignment: caregiver, single mom, financial planner, a Mimi without a Popi for our grandchildren, matriarch of our family, and yet it was mine just the same.

There have been many times that I have wrestled with the assignment, instead of resting. Let me assure you the wrestling only wasted time and much needed energy. While in a desert we must conserve energy, because we do not know how far it is until we find the next oasis. When faced with a difficult decision, weigh your true options, seek good counsel from someone who is familiar with your circumstances, pray and ask God's wisdom and guidance, and then make the best possible decision. When you put the decision into action – rest in it. Do not look back and second guess; go forward, for there is no other way to get through a desert but forward. Do not allow past regrets to haunt you. We all have them. Learn from them, but do not allow them to define you and terrify you forever. Forgive yourself and move on in freedom.

The next letter in the acrostic for trust is U: Unconditional love for God, even when I cannot understand His ways. This is one of the most difficult principles to accept. At first glance it appears that God does not care when we are hurting, that He is indifferent to our pain and suffering. After all He is God. He should just save us from all evil and make life stress free, right? Well, that was His original plan for His creation. But Adam and Eve decided to disobey and try it their way. Their choice resulted in God allowing each of us for all time to have a free will, the right to choose between good and evil. Since that time the world lives under a larger law of God: the law of sowing and reaping. God will not interfere with all the wrong actions of the people on the earth. He allows us freedom to make choices, this is true unconditional love. God does not make us do what is right. He shows us what is right, and allows us freedom to choose. With this freedom comes the law of sowing and reaping, and the corresponding consequences.

We must continually check our choices. We must ask ourselves: "How will this decision affect those around me? Will it hurt my family or other generations that will follow?" Do I take my responsibilities seriously? For example:

• Voting: Do I take my civic duties with thoughtful consideration?

• Character: Am I more concerned about what people think of me or what God thinks of me?

• Standing for what is right: While not everyone is called to be a crusader, we all have a responsibility to make our voices heard for moral issues that affect our communities, families and workplaces.

• Honesty at work: Would people be surprised to discover that I am a Christian? Do my Christian principles govern my work ethics as well?

• Defending values: As one who has experienced God's mercy and grace, have you ever come to the aid of another person who has been mistreated or taken advantage of? Have you risked your reputation to do the right thing?

To trust God one must unconditionally love Him because of His character, and believe He does balance justice through love, mercy and grace.

The next letter in the word trust is S, which stands for Surrender. I must learn to surrender my will to His. The word surrender just seems to pierce the heart of a true champion. It is not easy to surrender something to God, placing the outcome of everything into His hands. We must come to the place of admitting that He is God and knows best. It sounds ridiculous that we consider ourselves more competent than God, yet our actions say this every time we insist on doing things our way, not His. He gave us laws to live by to protect us. not to keep us from pleasure. If we could learn the discipline of surrender we would live longer and be more peaceful while we were living.

I challenge you to choose one concern in your life and surrender it to God right now. Some things you can hand over to Him in your mind, by mentally giving Him the problem. Or you may have to do what I did a few years ago with my adult children. I laid each of their pictures on the floor placing my hand on their photo. I then prayed for God to take care of them, guide them and to help me release them as adults for His care and protection from this moment on. I have been tempted from time to time to take those cares back, but realized pretty quickly that He was far more qualified and in the end surrendered them back to Him.

The final letter is T for Timing – God's not mine. A large part of trust in God is learning to wait for God to guide you. The key word being wait. I must admit I am a get it done myself kind of gal. I tend to run not walk when beginning a project, so in the past I would see waiting as wasting time. Now I have a better understanding about waiting. It is proactive, not passive at all. Here are a few things that I do when God requires me to wait for something that I want right now!

I pray about the idea, need or task.

I seek godly counsel from trusted friends or mentors

I get things ready for the moment God gives me the go ahead

I wait expectantly for Him to act in a supernatural way.

Waiting for God to pave the way for me has never been a waste of time, let me assure you. He can do more in a moment than you could do in your own strength and knowledge in a lifetime. Remember the vast Universe he spoke into existence? He can take care of any problem if we hand it over to Him willingly.

Once you have established trust and confidence in God, you can rely on His knowledge to get you through anything! But there will be temptations along the way to alter His instructions and do it your way. When we become fatigued, there is a desire to take a short-cut, to try and find an easier way. Short-cuts usually end up being costly. They look good, but end up taking longer.

I have found that when people go through extremely difficult times they will turn to something to get relief. There is only one who knows all and can be there with you 24/7. This is God, great and good, the one in whom you can place your faith in with absolute confidence. You just have to give Him your T.R.U.S.T. He is above extraordinary. Just realize, in our human finite thinking, we are limited in knowing just how truly *out of the ordinary God is!*

"Blessed is the man who trusts in the Lord, whose confidence is in him. He will be like a tree planted by the water that sends out its roots by the stream."
(Jeremiah 17:7-8a)

In Closing

Expect Struggles to Attain Extraordinary

Difficulties and obstacles are the challenges we must go through to attain life beyond ordinary. When hindrances confront us we must recognize them as opportunities to prove what we are made of. It is easy to move forward on a journey if the road is a four lane expressway with no bumps, curves, or detours to slow us down. But when faced with impassable roadblocks, if we persevere at the point of conflict, we will develop the character to wear the crown of success with true grace and honor. The greatest things are always hedged about by the hardest things. So, determine now, what price you are willing to pay to move past living an ordinary life. Never give up on your dreams, seeing them fulfilled lies imbedded in the very heart of those hardships and trails that are pressing you this very hour, week or month of your life. Remember, obstacles never announce themselves or come at a good time, just know they will come.

Your knowledge of these steps to extraordinary will do you no good unless you decide to do them. Make the decision to do these and whatever else you must do to live a life above ordinary! Live extraordinary, and you will never regret it!

Pamala is available for:

Retreat and Conference Speaking

See website for possible speaking topics for your group.

Life Coaching

Why use trial and error in planning your life and pursuing your dreams?

Pamala will help navigate and motivate you to continue pursuing and achieving your personal best!

Contact Information

www.livingextraordinarytoday.com

pamala777@yahoo.com